THE CHANGING ROOM

THE CHANGING ROOM
更衣室

Selected poetry of
Zhai Yongming
翟永明

Translated from Chinese by
Andrea Lingenfelter

Zephyr Press & The Chinese University Press of Hong Kong
Brookline, Mass. | Hong Kong

Cover image by Xu Bing
Book design by *type*slowly
Printed in Hong Kong

This publication is supported by the Jintian Literary Foundation. Zephyr Press
also acknowledges with gratitude the financial support of The National
Endowment for the Arts and the Massachusetts Cultural Council.

massculturalcouncil.org

ART WORKS.
arts.gov

Zephyr Press, a non-profit arts and education 501(c)(3) organization,
publishes literary titles that foster a deeper understanding of cultures
and languages. Zephyr books are distributed to the trade in the U.S.
and Canada by Consortium Book Sales and Distribution [www.cbsd.com]
and by Small Press Distribution [www.spdbooks.org].

Cataloguing-in publication data is available from the Library of Congress.

Published for the rest of the world by:
The Chinese University Press
The Chinese University of Hong Kong
Sha Tin, N.T., Hong Kong

ZEPHYR PRESS
www.zephyrpress.org

JINTIAN
www.jintian.net

THE CHINESE UNIVERSITY PRESS
www.chineseupress.com

CONTENTS

INTRODUCTION
Wang Ping

It can be hard to be a woman, but it's even harder to be a Chinese woman poet who has survived drastically different eras in Chinese modern history: the Cultural Revolution, "educated youth" in the countryside, post Cultural Revolution, Misty School (*Menglongshi*), New York City diaspora, and China's current economic reform and boom. Zhai Yongming has lived through all these historical eras, and her poetry vibrates with an energy born out of the tumult.

My first encounter with Zhai Yongming's poems came when I was studying at Beijing University in the early 1980s. At that time, Beijing University was launching waves of heated debates on freedom of speech in relation to the "Democracy Wall" in Beijing, and the "Star" salon launched China's contemporary art movement. Bei Dao, Gu Cheng, Yang Lian, Jiang He, Mang Ke and Yan Li (also a Star member), started *Jintian (Today)* poetry magazine in the late '70s, which pushed Chinese poetry into a new movement with its "misty" or "obscure" imagery and new voices. After *Jintian* was banned in 1980, their poems spread even more quickly among college students and poetry lovers. Zhai's poems were perhaps the most representative of this school: dark, heavy, collage-like imagery that reflected the influence of French Imagism. But what made Zhai's poetry really stand out was the fluidity and persistence through the complex maze of her interior world—a world filled with darkness, water, moon, mystery, courage and a will to live with dignity, grace, and beauty.

In 1989, Allen Ginsberg brought a group of poets to New York for the first Chinese-American Poetry Festival. When he recruited me as a translator and interpreter for the event, I was excited about the opportunity to translate the works of Bei Dao, Yang Lian, Gu Cheng, and especially Zhai Yongming, but for some reason her name wasn't on the program list. Only Shu Ting was there to represent all women poets from China.

Soon after this event I started my own translation project: *New Generation: Poetry from China Today*, an anthology of contemporary Chinese poets. I originally planned on including the earliest Misty School poets, but met with great difficulties for a number of reasons, so I instead began with the Post-misty school writers, also known as the New Generation or Third Generation. Zhai Yongming was my first choice. I paired her with Anne Waldman, a poet and performer from the so-called New York School. If Zhai Yongming represented the yin—feminine, moon, water, then Ann Waldman would be the yang—fire, sun . . . Though I had never met Zhai, I sensed the power lurking between and within her words, and Anne, a true Leo, could amplify this energy while her own yin side was released through translating Zhai's work. I made a first draft, sent it to Anne, then met with Anne in New York to work out the details. It was invariably a hot and humid summer afternoon. Perhaps Zhai's mystical images and fluid sounds were simply too complex to be conveyed into English. Anne was completely frustrated throughout the session, and it took several rounds of follow-up emails before we finally reached a version that began to satisfy us both.

I finally met Zhai in 1993 in Chengdu, on my way to Lhasa with poet Lewis Warsh. Her beauty and grace were truly shocking, but what struck me the most was the power that graced her face and body, the spirit that sprang from her eyes. Lewis had an instant crush on her, and didn't stop talking about her for the entire trip all the way back to New York. She was very quiet, listening with a smile as her friends, the other poets from Chengdu (Ouyang Jianghe, Xiaoxiao, Wan Xia) chattered and argued loudly over spicy Sichuan hotpot. When she did speak, everyone stopped and listened. Her words were few, but precise and layered with many aftertastes, just like her poetry. This encounter confirmed every impression I had gathered from reading her poetry.

Zhai Yongming later moved to New York City with her husband, the painter He Duoling. We were able to meet and talk at quite a few gatherings at *Yihang* events—a poetry journal founded by Yan Li. She was even quieter at these events, as she didn't speak much English, and most of the conversation rattled along in English. I was happy just to sit next to her, feeling both her grace and frustration. At the time He Duoling's art was being shown at various galleries throughout the U.S. Her media was poetry, but not many of her poems had been translated into English. There were many Chinese poets, artists, and musicians living in New York then—Tan Dun, Ai Weiwei, Yan Li, Yao Chingzhang, Peng Bangzhen, Wang Yu—but this was a different land, different people, and a lifestyle completely alien from her home in Chengdu. She grew slightly more pale and reticent each time I saw her, until one day she told me that she would be taking a trip through America's West, then going home. There was a new glow in her eyes, and her face was beginning to regain its color. I was certainly sorry to see her go, but happy that she was returning to her roots. New York had changed her fundamentally. I couldn't pinpoint exactly what, and I don't think even she knew, but we both knew a transformation was brewing. It might take a while, but it would happen.

We exchanged a few quick emails after she went home. Most of the news came from mutual friends. She and her husband split up. She opened White Nights café. For a second, I wondered if she had "plunged into the sea," a euphemism for those who abandoned their previous profession to become business people, a tsunami that had swept the whole of China. But it only lasted for a second. Zhai Yongming would never abandon poetry.

Then one day in 2006, I opened the new edition of *Today* that Bei Dao had sent. The first poem that jumped out was *Chuji (Child Prostitute)* by Zhai Yongming. I read it, then read it again and again as tears streaked down my face. It was a devastating poem about a little girl kidnapped and forced into prostitution. By the time her father found her, she was half dead. The voice definitely belonged to Zhai Yongming—dark, hauntingly beautiful, but it was also the voice of a lioness that had come out of her maze and was now roaring with indignation and grace, for all the sentient beings who cannot or have no means to speak. Her journey from interior to exterior, from self to the world, from yin to yang, had finally come full circle. And she continues to develop as a woman, as a Chinese woman poet. In this new book of translations, Zhai has expanded and fused herself with a universal image of woman through compassion, passion, and wisdom. This book is a diamond.

TRANSLATOR'S FOREWORD
Andrea Lingenfelter

Zhai Yongming's poetry first came to me around 1990 in a manila envelope, bundled with poems by a handful of other writers. The other poems in the group didn't leave a deep impression on me, but Zhai Yongming's poems ("Premonition," "Longing," and "Abandoned House," all from her 1984 sequence, "Woman") were a revelation. The only post-Mao poetry by a woman that I'd seen at that point was Shu Ting's. Moody, full of hurt, and tender, Shu Ting's work challenged the relentlessly extroverted political boosterism of Socialist Realism; and yet the poet's persona fit neatly into a traditional feminine mold: the long-suffering, melancholy victim of Fate. But when I read Zhai Yongming, I was struck by the acuity of her perceptions and the intensity of her voice. Zhai's persona projected anger and self-assertion, as if she were reclaiming for herself something that had long been denied to her and other women. She closed the original version of "Abandoned House" with this declaration: "I am a woman."

I translated the three poems I had, one of which was soon published in the *Chicago Review*, but I had no other information on Zhai and few ideas, in the pre-Internet age, of how to find out more. Then I read Michelle Yeh's *Anthology of Modern Chinese Poetry* (1994) and was delighted to find Zhai's work included. I learned that she lived in Chengdu, Sichuan, and through a friend I obtained a copy of one her books, which became a primary source for a chapter of my dissertation. Michael Day's pioneering work was also helpful.

From the very outset, I knew I wanted to translate a book-length collection of Zhai's work, but until I could contact her and meet her, it would be hard to proceed. The opportunity to meet Zhai Yongming arrived in the early spring of 2006, when she came to the US for a conference. We were introduced by a mutual friend, and she readily granted me permission to translate her work. The next step was to find a publisher, and another friend and fellow translator introduced me to Christopher Mattison at Zephyr Press, who responded enthusiastically to the sample poems I showed him. The book you are holding in your hands was on its way.

Zhai Yongming was born to a military family in Chengdu, Sichuan in 1955 and began publishing poetry in 1981. In the 1970s, she spent time in the countryside as a sent-down youth, a formative experience that is a powerful presence in her early work, in sequences such as "Woman" and "Tranquil Village" (1985). Even now, decades on, the experience has lost little of its immediacy for her. She has also written about the trials of coming of age under Maoism in the essay, "Helpless Youth" (forthcoming in English from *Renditions*). Although a contemporary of the Misty Poets, she is generally thought of as a member of the Newborn Generation, the Misty Poets' successors. Zhai Yongming has also been categorized as a "stream of consciousness" poet by Michelle Yeh.[1] Like others in this group, she drew inspiration from the American confessional poets, especially Sylvia Plath. Plath's early influence is palpable, particularly in the groundbreaking 20-poem sequence "Woman," in which Zhai forcefully articulates women's subjective physical and social experiences of life.

While Zhai Yongming's poems from the 1980s owed much to Anglophone Confessional poets, even then Zhai's voice was unmistakably her own. With imagery dominated by night, darkness, blood, sex, and death, those early poems also directly engaged traditional Chinese cultural paradigms. Zhai's recasting of Chinese yin and yang cosmology along feminist lines was a dominant thread in a body of work that was otherwise intensely personal and contemporary. Over time, she has continued to go back to China's literary and historical past, using it as a source of inspiration, as a counterpoint to modern experience, and as part of an ongoing dialogue with patriarchal Confucian historiography. These lines from "Premonition" illustrate her reframing of yin and yang:

> Enormous birds peer down at me from the sky
> With human eyes

---

[1] Along with Lu Yimin 陆忆敏 (b. 1962), Zhang Zhen 张真 (b. 1961), Yi Lei 伊蕾 (b. 1951), Tang Yaping 唐亚平 (b. 1962), Wang Xiaoni 王小妮 (b. 1955), Liu Manliu 刘漫流 (b. 1962), Meng Lang 孟浪 (b. 1961), Bei Ling 贝岭 (b. 1959), and Xi Chuan 西川 (b. 1963).

In a barbarous atmosphere that keeps its secrets
Winter lets its brutally male consciousness rise and fall.

I've always been uncommonly serene
Like the blind, I see night's darkness in the light of day

那些巨大的鸟从空中向我俯视
带着人类的眼神
在一种秘而不宣的野蛮空气中
冬天起伏着残酷的雄性意识

我一向有着不同寻常的平静
犹如盲者，因此我在白天看见黑夜

Zhai elaborated her ideas in the preface to the first edition of "Woman,"
an essay entitled "Black Night Consciousness," which opens:

Now is the moment when at last I've become powerful. Or perhaps I
should say that now I've finally become aware of the world around me
and of the implications of my place in it. An individual and universal in-
ner consciousness—I call this Black Night Consciousness—has ordained
that I be the bearer of female (*nüxing*) consciousness, beliefs, and feel-
ings, and that I will directly take that charge upon myself, and put it into
what I see as the best work I can do on behalf of that consciousness.
Namely, poetry.

As one half of humanity, from the moment of her birth, a female faces
a completely different world. Her first glimpse of this world is of course
colored by her individual spirit and sensibility, and possibly even by a
psychology of private resistance.

More than anything, what Zhai asserts here is her imperative to write
from her own singular and unique point of view. This individuality is
grounded in her psychosexual and socio-cultural awareness of herself

as a woman. Nonetheless, Zhai does not claim to speak for all women, although judging by the impact that "Woman" made on other Chinese women poets, a number of them thought that she did. Zhai Yongming appears to have underestimated the universality of her poetry and her point of view (at least among women), and she was not comfortable with the overwhelming response to the "Woman" cycle and its preface.

Zhai described the craze for her as a "black whirlwind" (hei xuanfeng 黑 旋风) that swept over China during the second half of the 1980s, and she was taken aback by the appearance of a crowd of imitators. In March of 1989, she wrote an article, published in the June issue of Poetry Monthly (Shikan) in which she commented on this trend: "As a joke I often say that I should change the first line of 'The Black Room' from 'All crows under Heaven are black' to 'All women under Heaven are black.'" Tellingly, she also revised the final line of "Abandoned House" from "I am a woman" to "I am myself" sometime between its original publication (in 1984) and 1994, when she reprinted it in another collection. Whatever her reservations about being thrust into the public eye as a speaker for all women, Zhai has not abandoned her identity as a feminist. In an interview she granted me a few years back, she told me she rejected the "taboo" against feminism (nüxingzhuyi) in contemporary China and had no difficulty calling herself a feminist.

The early 1990s were a time of crisis for many Chinese poets in Zhai's circle, and a number gave up writing poetry. Zhai continued to write. The poems from this period explore her interior world, although scenes that touch on her extended stay in New York City also figure into a number of pieces. By the late 1990s, Zhai had fully re-engaged with the outside world and with history, and was further exploring the lives of other women artists. Her poetry, while still personal, was less about defining her own identity and more about locating her place in a historical and cultural context.

One of the earliest poems in which she showed a renewed and positive engagement with the past and Chinese tradition was the 1999 poem "Climbing the Heights on the Double Ninth" (translated in this volume). Written on the occasion of a Chinese holiday that dates back thousands of years and about which many poems were written in antiquity, this poem illustrates the immediacy of the cultural past and its relevance to the present for Zhai.

The poem has a colophon from a poem by Wang Wei (701–761 CE) about the Double Ninth and the sadness of missing friends and family. Climbing to a height and thinking of friends and loved ones is a common trope in classical poetry, and Zhai makes it her own, bringing the situation to life in our time:

Today I raise a cup alone   while River and mountains change color
The green months of spring depleted me
This figure, "Nine Nine"   is once again
Reborn in my veins

今朝我一人把盏　江山变色
青色三春消耗了我
九九这个数字　如今又要
轮回我的血脉

Similarly, Zhai's poem about Frida Kahlo, "Scissorhands' Dialogue," is at once a rumination on Kahlo's life and a highly personal reflection on Zhai's life—and, by extension, the lives of all women artists:

"For beauty, women bleed in secret"

They bleed but who cares:
The scissors in her heart are cutting
Love's true outlines   she stares
Eyes sharp as an animal's
Two legs scissoring   hissing, hissing

. . .

In the darkness   my legs extended
Dancing with Kahlo
"Women: coming and going
Burning away your essence like candles"

"为了美，女人暗暗淌血"

淌血　谁会在乎：
她心中的剪刀正在剪
一个爱的真轮廓　她注视
动物之眼一样犀利
两腿绞动着　发出嘶嘶声

. . .

在黑暗中　我的腿脚伸出
与卡洛跳舞
"女人们：来，去
蜡烛般烧毁自己的本性"

These interests have remained central to Zhai's poetry over the past decade, with a number of pieces in her 2008 collection, "Pretty Words," treating the past as a counterpoint to the present. Using classical themes and images such as homesickness, leave-taking, and letters from home, Zhai contrasts their modern and ancient manifestations, pointing to differences and similarities in lived experience during different periods in history.

Her long-standing concern for women artists and poets has evolved into a revisionist historicism. She has been researching the lives of poets like Yu Xuanji and Xue Tao, along with historical figures like Yang Guifei, Zhao Feiyan, and Yu Ji, in an effort to restore their reputations. In doing so, she is taking on both the conclusions of generations of Confucian historians as well as the unexamined contemporary cultural attitudes that have grown out of them. "The Song of Historical Beauties" revisits the traditional verdicts on Yang Guifei, Zhao Feiyan, and Yu Ji, concluding that:

> At first they praise a woman for her beauty
> But at other times
> When catastrophe looms
> When cities erupt in flames
> Men, oh men
> Delight in denouncing women for their crimes"

> 开始把女人叫作尤物
> 而在另外的时候
> 当大祸临头
> 当城市开始燃烧
> 男人呵男人
> 乐于宣告她们的罪状"

More recent history concerns Zhai as well, as in "Fourteen Plainsongs" (about her mother's youth during the Communist Revolution), "The Language of the '50s" (which contrasts her generation's experience versus that of contemporary youth), and "The Testament of Hu Huishan," which memorializes one of the young victims of the May 2008 earthquake in Sichuan.

As her international reputation has grown, Zhai has traveled widely to participate in literary gatherings. I have chosen one of the poems that came out of a 2009 trip to India for a meeting of Chinese and Indian writers to close this collection.

I could not have completed this project without the gracious help and encouragement of Zhai Yongming herself, who has shown me around Chengdu, taking me to sites like the Han dynasty irrigation project at Dujiangyan and the Tang woman poet Xue Tao's retreat, Wangjiang lou, all the while placing everything we were looking at in a larger context. She has also treated me to many memorably wonderful meals in Chengdu and Beijing. I'd like to thank my editor at Zephyr, Christopher Mattison, who has shepherded this project through several relocations, both his and mine, across oceans, down coastlines and across town; but who intrepidly sorted through what in the end amounted to hundreds of pages of English translations and Chinese originals, giving excellent feedback and suggestions, reviewing and putting in my many revisions, and painstakingly going over corrections with me. I owe thanks to Heather McHugh, who read an early version of this manuscript and offered valuable comments, which I took to heart and which pushed me to bring these translations to the next level. Other friends and colleagues who have offered support and constructive criticism include Steve Bradbury, who introduced me to Zephyr and whose insightful suggestions helped me reshape the early poems into their current form, Jennifer Feeley, who generously made me copies of some of Zhai's early works from rare or out of print books, Huang Yibing for making the initial introduction to Zhai, Wang Ching-hsien (Yang Mu), who gave me the green light to write about Zhai in my dissertation and thus gave me the space to examine her works in depth, Michelle Yeh, whose knowledge and expertise have enriched my understanding of Zhai and her contexts, and lastly to all of the editors who have responded enthusiastically to these works over the years and who have published them in literary journals. I dedicate this book to my children Oona, Isaiah, and Eleni.

THE CHANGING ROOM
更衣室

预感

穿黑裙的女人夤夜而来
她秘密的一瞥使我精疲力竭
我突然想起这个季节鱼都会死去
而每条路正在穿越飞鸟的痕迹

貌似尸体的山峦被黑暗拖曳
附近灌木的心跳隐约可闻
那些巨大的鸟从空中向我俯视
带着人类的眼神
在一种秘而不宣的野蛮空气中
冬天起伏着残酷的雄性意识

我一向有着不同寻常的平静
犹如盲者，因此我在白天看见黑夜
婴儿般直率，我的指纹
已没有更多的悲哀可提供
脚步！正在变老的声音
梦显得若有所知，从自己的眼睛里
我看到了忘记开花的时辰
给黄昏施加压力

藓苔含在口中，他们所恳求的意义
把微笑会心地折入怀中
夜晚似有似无地痉挛，像一声咳嗽
憋在喉咙，我已离开这个死洞

PREMONITION

A woman dressed in black arrives in the dead of night
Just one secretive glance leaves me spent
I realize with a start: this is the season when all fish die
And every road is criss-crossed with traces of birds in flight

A corpse-like chain of mountain ranges dragged off by the darkness
The heartbeats of nearby thickets barely audible
Enormous birds peer down at me from the sky
With human eyes
In a barbarous atmosphere that keeps its secrets
Winter lets its brutally male consciousness rise and fall.

I've always been uncommonly serene
Like the blind, I see night's darkness in the light of day
Artless as an infant, my fingerprints
Can reveal no more grief
Footsteps! A sound now growing old
Dreams seem to possess some knowledge, and with my own eyes
I saw an hour that forgot to blossom
Pressing down on the dusk.

Fresh moss in their mouths, the meanings they sought
Folded their smiles back into their breasts in tacit understanding
The night seems to shudder, like a cough
Stuck in the throat, I've already quit this dead end hole.

荒屋

那里有深紫色台阶
那里植物是红色的太阳鸟
那里石头长出人脸

我常常从那里走过
以各种紧张的姿态
我一向在黄昏时软弱
而那里荒屋闭紧眼睛
我站在此地观望
看着白昼痛苦的光从它身上流走

念念有词，而心忑忑
脚步绕着圈，从我大脑中走过
房顶射出传染性的无名悲痛
像一个名字高不可攀
像一件礼物孤芳自赏和一幅画
像一块散发着高贵品质的玻璃死气沉沉

那里一切有如谣言
那里有害热病的灯提供阴谋
那里后来被证明：无物可寻

我来了 我靠近 我侵入
怀着从不开敞的脾气
活得像一个灰瓮

它的傲慢日子仍然尘封未动
就像它是荒屋
我是我自己

ABANDONED HOUSE

There, the steps are a deep purple
There, the plants are red sunbirds
There, the stones have human faces

I often pass by there
In a variety of nervous postures
I've always been feeble come dusk
And that abandoned house shuts its eyes tight
As I stand and stare
Watching rays of daylight slide from its body in agony

Muttering to myself, my heart racing
My footsteps circle, while the nameless and contagious sorrow
Shooting from the rooftop passes through my brain
Like a name too lofty to reach
Like a gift savored in solitary splendor or a painting
Like a piece of glass sparkling with refinement but heavy with death

There, everything is like a rumor
And heatstruck lamps offer their conspiracies
There, it will be proven: nothing more will remain

I arrive   I approach   I trespass
Nursing a temperament I've never revealed
Living like an urn filled with ashes

Its proud days lie buried in dust, untouched
And just like this abandoned house
I am myself

渴望

今晚所有的光只为你照亮
今晚你是一小块殖民地
久久停留，忧郁从你身体内
渗出，带着细腻的水滴

月亮像一团光洁芬芳的肉体
酣睡，发出诱人的气息
两个白昼夹着一个夜晚
在它们之间，你黑色眼圈
保持着欣喜

怎样的喧嚣堆积成我的身体
无法安慰，感到有某种物体将形成
梦中的墙壁发黑
使你看见三角形泛滥的影子
全身每个毛孔都张开
不可捉摸的意义
星星在夜空毫无人性地闪耀
而你的眼睛装满
来自远古的悲哀和快意

带着心满意足的创痛
你优美的注视中，有着恶魔的力量
使这一刻，成为无法抹掉的记忆

DESIRE

Tonight all the lights are shining for you
Tonight you are a small colonial outpost
You've lingered here, and melancholy seeps
From your body, with tiny, perfect drops of water

Like a clean bright ball of scented flesh, the moon
Sleeps sweetly, each breath a seduction
A night squeezed between two days
And in their midst, the black orbs of your eyes
Still filled with joy

What kind of tumult was heaped together to shape my body
Beyond consolation, feeling like some substance about to take form
The walls in the dream turn black
Making you see the shadows overflowing the triangle
Every pore on your body opens up
Concepts you cannot grasp
Stars in the night sky glimmer inhumanly
But your eyes are flooded
With the sorrows and joys of antiquity

Bearing the wounds of contentment
Your beautiful gaze possesses a demonic power
That transforms this moment into a memory that can't be wiped away

边缘

傍晚六点钟，夕阳在你们
两腿之间燃烧
睁着精神病人的浊眼
你可以抗议，但我却饱尝
风的啜泣，一粒小沙并不起眼
注视着你们，它想说
鸟儿又在重复某个时刻的旋律

你们已走到星星的边缘
你们懂得沉默
两个名字的奇异领略了秋天
你们隐藏起脚步，使我
得不到安宁，蝙蝠在空中微笑
说着一种并非人类的语言

这个夜晚无法安排一个
更美好的姿态，你的头
靠在他的腿上，就象
水靠着自己的岩石
现在你们认为无限寂寞的时刻
将化为葡萄，该透明的时候透明
该破碎的时候破碎

瞎眼的池塘想望穿夜，月亮如同
猫眼，我不快乐也不悲哀
靠在已经死去的栅栏上注视你们
我想告诉你 没有人去拦阻黑夜
黑暗已进入这个边缘

MARGINS

Six in the evening, the setting sun blazes
Across your coupled limbs
Staring into the cloudy eyes of a madman
You could fight back, but I've had my fill of
The wind's sobbing, and no one will notice a grain of sand
Staring fixedly at the two of you, it's trying to say
The birds are once again repeating an old refrain

You two have walked to the margins of the stars
You know the meaning of silence
The strangeness of two names savoring autumn
You cover your tracks, denying me
Even a vestige of peace, while up in the sky grinning bats
Converse in a language not entirely human

You couldn't possibly make a prettier picture
Than you do tonight, your head
Pillowed on his lap, the way
Water is cradled by stones
Now you believe the loneliest moments
Will ripen into grapes, turning translucent when they should
                              turn translucent
Bursting when they should burst

The blinded pool wants to see right through the night, the moon like
A cat's eye, and I'm neither pleased nor aggrieved
Leaning against a dead fence and staring at you both
I want to tell you   No one is holding back the night
Darkness is already encroaching on these margins

旋转

并非只是太阳在旋转
沉沦早已开始，当我倒着出生
这挣扎如此恐怖，使我成形
保存这头朝地的事实我已长得这般大

我来的时候并不是一颗星
我站得很稳，路总在转
从东到西，无法逃脱圆圈的命运
够了，不久我的头被装上轨道
我亲眼注视着它向天空倾倒
并竭力保持自身的重量

大地压着我的脚，一个沉重的天
毁坏我，是那轮子在晕旋
天竺葵太象我的心，又细腻又热情
但我无法停下来，使它不再转
微笑最后到来，象一个致命的打击

夜还是白昼？全都一样
孵出卵石之眼和雌雄之躯
据说球茎花已开得一无所剩
但靠着那条路的边缘
黑色涡旋正茫茫无边

旋转又旋转，象一颗
飞舞着不祥事件的星
把我团团围住：但谁在你的外端？

REVOLVING

It's not just the sun that revolves
The sinking started long ago, when I was born, upside down
The struggle was terrifying, and it shaped me
Maintaining this face-down reality, I've grown to the age that I have

I was no star when I arrived
I stand very still, while the road twists and turns
From East to West, there's no escaping the circle of Fate
But enough of that, for soon my head will be put into orbit
With my own eyes I see it cast into the sky
Where it fights that weightlessness with all of its strength

Earth presses down onto my feet, a heavy sky
Destroys me, it's that wheel spinning
Geraniums are too much like my heart, hot-blooded and slim
But I can't stop, can't stop it from turning
And finally there's a smile, like a fatal blow

Night or day? It's all the same
An eye that hatches oval stones, male and female bodies
They say the kohlrabi has flowered and withered already
But at the edge of the road
Black whirlpools are spinning into infinity

Revolving and revolving, like an
Unlucky star dancing in the air
Round and round, encircling me, but who is on your outer surface?

第一月

——辛丑土
闲轸
春社: 二月十六日

仿佛早已存在, 仿佛早已就序
我走来, 声音概不由己
它把我安顿在朝南的厢房

第一次来我就赶上漆黑的日子
到处都有脸型相像的小径
凉风吹得我苍白寂寞
玉米地在这种时刻精神抖擞
我来到这里, 听到双鱼星的噪叫
又听见敏感的夜抖动不已

极小的草垛散布肃穆
脆弱唯一的云像孤独的野兽
蹑足走来, 含有坏天气的味道
如同与我相逢成为值得理解的内心

鱼竿在水面滑动, 忽明忽灭的油灯
热烈沙哑的狗吠使人默想
昨天巨大的风声似乎了解一切
不要容纳黑树
每个角落布置一次杀机
忍受布满人体的时刻
现在我可以无拘无束地成为月光

THE FIRST MONTH

Xinchou, Earth
Illness and early death
Spring Sacrifice to the Earth: February 16

As if it had been there all along, as if by prior arrangement
I arrived, and a voice beyond my control
Placed me in a south-facing wing

I arrived just in time for the pitch black days
Every footpath looked the same
Breezes chilled me pale and lonely
While the cornfields pulsed with energy
When I arrived, I heard the roaring of Pisces
And the endless trembling of the sensitive night

Tiny haystacks spread out in a solemn array
One feeble cloud, like a solitary wild animal
Moved in on tiptoe, with a taste of foul weather
As if meeting me gave it a heart to match its shape

Fishing poles gliding over the water, flickering oil lamps
Fierce and ragged, the barking of dogs plunges me into thought
Yesterday's howling wind seemed to comprehend everything
To say nothing of those black trees
Murderous traps are set in every corner
I've endured the moment that covered my body
And can now become moonlight, unfettered

已婚夫妇梦中听见卯时雨水的声音
黑驴们靠着石磨商量明天
那里，阴阳混合的土地
对所有年月了如指掌

我听见公鸡打鸣
又听见轱辘打水的声音

A husband and wife hear the sound of pre-dawn rain in their dreams
Black donkeys lean against a millstone, talking about tomorrow
There, the soil where yin and yang intermingle
Knows each year by heart

I hear a cock's crow
And a windlass drawing water from a well

Xinchou refers to a time in the traditional Chinese calendar, spanning
the first and second months of the lunar year, from Xiaohan in the first
month to Lichun in the second month (1月 小寒到 2月 立春)

第二月

从早到午，走遍整个村庄
我的脚听从地下的声音
让我到达沉默的深度

无论走到哪家门前，总有人站着
端着饭碗，有人摇着空空的摇篮
走过一堵又一堵墙，我的脚不着地
荒屋在那里穷凶极恶，积着薄薄红土
是什么挡住我如此温情的视线？
在蚂蚁的必死之路
脸上盖着树叶的人走来
向日葵被割掉头颅. 粗糙糜烂的脖子
伸在天空下如同一排谎言
蓑衣装扮成神，夜里将作恶多端

寒食节出现的呼喊
村里人因抚慰死者而自我克制
我寻找，总带着未遂的笑容
内心伤口与他们的肉眼连成一线
怎样才能进入静安庄
尽管每天都有溺婴尸体和服毒的新娘

他们回来了，花朵列成纵队反抗
分娩的声音突然提高
感觉落日从里面崩溃
我在想：怎样才能进入
这时鸦雀无声的村庄

THE SECOND MONTH

From dawn to noon, I cover the whole village on foot
My steps obeying a voice from beneath the ground
That brings me to the very depths of silence

No matter whose gate I come to, someone is standing there
With a rice bowl in their hands, and someone is rocking an empty cradle
Passing wall after wall, my feet don't touch the ground
The abandoned houses there, boundless in their cruelty, coated in fine red dust
What blocks my sympathetic gaze?
On a path where ants are sure to die
People are walking, their faces covered with leaves
All of the sunflowers have had their heads lopped off. Their coarse, defiled necks
Stretch beneath the sky like a row of lies
A cape made of straw masquerades as a god, ready for a night of wicked deeds

Shouts ring out during the Cold Food festival
To comfort the dead, the villagers exercise restraint
I keep searching, wearing my ever-failing smile
The wound in my heart is strung on the same thread as their naked eyes
How can I ever be part of Tranquil Village?
Each day brings more drowned babies and brides who swallow poison

They've come back, and the flowers line up in formation, ready to resist
Suddenly, the sounds of childbirth grow louder
I feel the setting sun implode
I wonder: how can I ever be part of
This village where even the birds are silent

第五月

这是一个充满怀疑的日子，她来到此地
月亮露出凶光，繁殖令人心碎的秘密

走在黑暗中，夜光磷磷，天然无饰
她使白色变得如此分明
许多夜晚重新换过，她的手
放在你胸前依然神秘
蚕豆花细心地把静安庄吃掉
他人的入睡芬芳无比

在水一方，有很怪的树轻轻冷笑
有人叹息无名，她并不介意
进入你活生生的身体
使某些东西成形，它们是活的？
痛苦的树在一夜间改变模样
麦田守望人惊异
波动的土地使自己的根彻底消失

她去，她来，带着虚幻的风度
硕大无朋的石榴
从拐角两边的矮墙
露出内在淫欲的颜色
缓缓走动，憎恨所有的风
参与各种事物的恶毒，她一向如此
早已变成不明之物
甘美倾心的声音在你心内
其它失眠者的五月，因想到
扶乩的咒语，微微泛起不自觉的怯意

THE FIFTH MONTH

This is a day full of suspicion, she has arrived at this place
And the moon reveals its savage light, seeding heartrending secrets

Walking in the dark, the phosporescent night, natural and unadorned
She makes the whiteness well-defined
So many nights, one after another, her hands
On your chest keep their mystery
Broadbean flowers are eating up Tranquil Village with great care
Falling asleep is incomparably sweet for others

Along the river, a strange tree sneering faintly
Someone sighs at anonymity, but she doesn't mind
Entering your living body
Gives certain things a shape; are they alive?
A suffering tree alters its appearance overnight
The scarecrow guarding the wheat fields is startled
His roots have disappeared beneath the heaving earth

She goes, she returns, with a dream-like quality
At the corner of two low walls
A gigantic pomegranate
Displays its lusty colors
Walking languidly, despising all the winds
With a hand in all kinds of evil, she's always been like this
The tender and intimate voice in your heart
Grew faint long ago
For the other insomniacs, in the fifth month, recalling
Planchette and incantations spreads an unconscious fear

第十二月

如今已到离开静安庄的时候
牝马依然敲响它的黑蹄
西北风吹过无人之境
使一群牛犊想起战争……

迄今无法证明空虚的形体
落日象瘟疫降临，坐在村头
内心疮痍如一棵树
双手布置白色树液的欲望，被你唤醒

我抬头看见飞碟，偶然出现
偷偷抚摸怀中之石，临别与我接吻
整个村庄蒙受你的阴沉
鞋子装满沙粒，空气密布麦芽气味

太阳又高又冷
努力想成为有脑髓的生物
年迈的妇女翻动痛苦的鱼
每个角落，人头骷髅装满尘土
脸上露出干燥的微笑，晃动的黑影

步行的声音来自地底，如血液流动
蝴蝶们看见自己投奔死亡的模样
与你相似，距离是所有事物的中心
在地面上，我仍是异乡的孤身人

始终在这个鸦雀无声的村庄
耳听此时出生的古老喉音
肋骨隐隐作痛
一度可接近的时间为我打开黑夜的大门

THE TWELFTH MONTH

The time has come for me to leave Tranquil Village
The mare still stamps her black hooves
The northwest wind blows across this no-man's land
Reminding the herd of calves of war . . .

At this point there's no way to confirm the shape of emptiness
The setting sun descends like pestilence, sitting over the village
My heart wounded like a tree,
My hands arranging the desire of white sap. Awakened by your calls

I look up and see a flying saucer, it appears out of nowhere
Furtively caresses the stone in my breast, kisses me good-bye
The whole village has put up with your moodiness,
Shoes filled with grains of sand, the air thick with the scent of wheat grass

The sun is high and cold
Wishing with all its heart it could become a sentient being
An old woman turns over a fish that's in agony
In every corner, human skulls full of dust
Parched smiles on their faces, trembling shadows

The sound of footsteps comes from underground, flowing like blood
Butterflies see how they look in their flight from death
Like you, distance lies at the center of everything
Here on this ground, I'm still in a strange land

All along in this village where even the sparrows are silent
I've heard the ancient guttural sound born in this moment
Ribs secretly aching
An interval of approachable time opens for me the immense gate of night

女孩子站在暮色里
灰色马、灰色人影
石板被踢起的火花照亮
一种恶心感觉象雨淋在屋顶
婴儿的苦闷产生
我们离开
带着无法揣测的血肉之躯

归根结蒂，我到过这里
讨人喜欢
我走的时候却不怀好意
被烟熏出眼泪，目光朝向
伤了元气的轮回部分和古老的皱纹

低飞的鸟穿过内心使我一无所剩
刻着我出生日期的老榆树
又结满我父亲年龄的旧草绳
因给予我们生命而骄傲

村里的人站在向阳的斜坡上
对白昼怀疑，又绕尽远路回到夜里休息
老年人深深的目光使布满恶意的冬天撤退

使我强有力的脸上出现裂痕
最先看见魔术的孩子站在树下
他仍在思索
所有一切是怎样变出来的
在那些看不见的时刻

A girl is standing in the dusk
Gray horse, gray human shadows
Flagstones illuminated by kicked up sparks
Nausea, like rain pattering on the rooftop
The depressing birthing of a baby
We are leaving
Taking with us our unfathomable flesh and blood

In the end you could say I came here
Eager to please,
Now I'm leaving, my good will spent
Smoke brings tears to my eyes, my gaze turns inward
Dispirited bits of samsara and ancient wrinkles

Low-flying birds bore through my heart and leave me empty
The old elm with my birth date carved into it
Bound once more with hemp ropes as old as my father
Is prideful because it gave us life

The villagers stand on the south-facing slope
Suspicious of daytime, taking the long way around again, back to
                    their evening rest
The elders' profound gazes send winter's malice into retreat

Leaving cracks in my strong face.
The first thing I saw was a magical child standing beneath a tree
He's wondering still
How all of this came to be
During these unseen moments

黑房间

天下乌鸦一般黑，至此
我感到胆怯，它们有如此多的
亲戚，它们人多势众，难以抗拒

我们却必不可少，我们姐妹三人
婷婷玉立，来回踱步
胜券在握的模样
我却有意使坏，内心刻薄
表面保持当女儿的好脾气
重蹈每天的失败

待字闺中，我们是名门淑女
悻悻地微笑，挖空心思
使自己变得多姿多采
年轻，貌美，如火如荼
炮制很黑，很专心的圈套
（哪些牙齿磨利，目光笔直的好人
毫无起伏的面容是我的姐夫？）

我感到
我们的房间危机四伏
在夜晚，猫和老鼠都醒着
我们去睡，在梦中寻找陌生的门牌号码
在夜晚，我们是瓜熟蒂落的女人
颠鸾倒凤，如此等等

我们姐妹三人，我们日新月异
婚姻，依然是择偶的中心
卧室的光线使新婚夫妇沮丧
孤注一掷，我对自己说
"家是出发的地方"

THE BLACK ROOM

All crows under Heaven are equally black, and this
Fills me with fear, they have so many
Relatives, their numbers are legion, they're hard to resist

But we're indispensable, we three sisters
Slim and graceful, we glide to and fro
Looking like winners
But I intend to make mischief, I'm cruel at heart
Keeping up the appearance of a sweet-tempered daughter
My footsteps retrace my daily defeats

Awaiting proposals in our boudoirs, we young ladies of good family
Smile resentfully, racking our brains
For ways to enhance our charms
Youthful, beautiful, like fires ablaze
Seared black, single-minded snares
(Which of these good men with well-sharpened teeth, an unwavering gaze
And a steady expression will be my brother-in-law?)

I sense
Our chamber beset on all sides
At night, cats and mice alike are stirring
And we go to sleep, searching our dreams for unknown house numbers
At night, we women are like ripe melons ready to fall from the vine
Conjugal bliss, and all of that

We three sisters, different with each new day
Marriage, still the crux of finding a mate
Lights in the bedroom fill newlyweds with disappointment
Risk it all on one throw, I tell myself
"Home is where the journey begins"

白色的走廊

我见过白色的小小走廊
在不眠之夜移动
衣裙吹皱沙沙作响的风
小小的血滴开着花
象很多签名　单单调调的存在

我见过玉体横陈的病女孩
把美貌的头转动
她高烧的理由把夏天的温度破坏
我跑过失踪的门
那儿半开半闭的胸膛
把内心的嚣张变成
一些活生生的愿望

我见过孤独的小小走廊
穿白罩衫的女人悄悄走来
她哭泣的声音传得很远
母亲沾满血迹的两手忽隐忽现
在我眼中逡巡
让我担负起一个下午
手术刀的光芒
以及密密缝合的光线

我见过母亲的小小走廊
在黑暗中惊醒
似水的生命力把我轻轻托起
这是被迫出逃的方式
这是纯洁的小小走廊
分裂的方式　拖着我
病体有如梦中的百草园

WHITE CORRIDOR

I've seen a small white passage
Flickering on sleepless nights
Gusty winds rustle and wrinkle my skirts
Droplets of blood flowering
Like the humdrum existence   of so many signatures

I've seen a sickly girl pale as jade draped across the bed
She turns her pretty face from side to side
Her fever's wellsprings shatter the summer heat
I run past a vanished door
Where a half-opened chest cavity
Has turned an arrogant heart
Into vital hopes

I've seen a lonely little passage
A woman in a white coat walking quietly in
The sound of her weeping carries
Mother's blood-covered hands appear and disappear
Wavering before my eyes
Placing on me the burden of the afternoon
The brilliance of the scalpel
Tightly stitched rays of light

I've seen my mother's small passage
Awakened into darkness with a start
A life force like water gently held me up
That's how I was chased out
That's how a small, immaculate passage
Was rent apart   and I was pulled out
A sickly body has a botanical garden that's like a dream

栖息着多种多样的疫疾
没有来龙去脉
没有困倦
眼睁睁看着白衣的裂纹
充满魔力
夏天的病女孩摸索着走来
温顺的　雪白的凝眸
带着扫荡一切的幻觉

A host of diseases has lodged there
Lacking origin or outcome
Indefatigable
Eyes stare at the rips in white clothing
Full of allure
The sickly girl of summer feels her way forward
Meek and mild   her snowy gaze
Holds a vision of everything swept clean

我的蝙蝠

蝙蝠是我的密友　是我的衣服
是我的头发追随我
隐姓埋名的缘由
漫长的冬天与我同住

他是畜类中最钟情的一种
空虚易碎的心最能打动
茫茫无边的鬼魂
悬空的夜晚　　有他的睡眠

蝙蝠是人的伙计　　无人知晓
深不可测的世界有我们全面的出发点
他古怪的脾气向来就强调
先天优势　　当清晨照射我们的住处
他偷偷离去
起先我以为他是懂事的飞禽
他激情的十指纠正错误
他解释　　又公布
那理所当然的区分

蝙蝠是我的影子
他的思想跟踪我
获取确切的情报　　直至
盲目的爱情使他神智恢复
孤零零的流浪
他执意的飞行永远无法接近鸟类
因他生就的苦难相难以自由
睡不着的夜里　　他倒挂着
与我作对　　加强四周的黑暗

MY BAT

Bat is my secret friend   the clothes I wear
The hair trailing behind me
The reason I go incognito
Abiding with me through endless winters

He's a notably devoted domestic animal
A fragile and empty heart is easiest to touch
A spirit that knows no limits
Nights suspended in the air   embrace his sleep

Bat serves us   no one is aware
Our point of origin is in the world's unfathomable depths
His eccentricity only confirms
His inborn superiority   When early morning shines into our dwelling
He slips away
At first I took him for some sort of wise bird
His zealous digits righting old wrongs
He explains   he broadcasts
Significant distinctions

Bat is my shadow
His mind tracks me
Gathering reliable intelligence   until
Blind love brings him back to his senses
Lonely wayfarer
His perserving flight will never match a bird's
For his look of inborn suffering is hard to escape
On sleepless nights   he hangs upside down
Opposing me   deepening the surrounding darkness

蝙蝠是古老的故事
是梦中最后的发现
是一个畸形的伪装的鸟
高贵的心难以着陆
他重大的　肉感的形态
始终与我有关
这一切幼时多么熟悉
现在也依然存在

Bat is an ancient story
The final sequence of a dream
A bird with strange camouflage
Such a lofty spirit can hardly come to earth
His weighty   carnal form
Has been linked to me from the start
The intimacy of our childhood
Remains unbroken even today

玩偶

当我厌倦了黑夜
常常从梦里坐起 开口说话
小小的玩偶闪着褐光
我说话 带着一种不真切的口吻
我说着一直想说的胡言乱语

像静物 也像黑暗中的灯泡
面目丑陋的玩偶不慌不忙
无法识别它内心的狂野
当我拧亮台灯 梦在纸上燃烧
我的梦多么心酸 思念我儿时的玩伴
躺在我手上，一针又一针
我缝着它的面孔和笑容

梦见未来的一夜 它开口说话
来到我的床边
白色的床 分开阴阳两界
白色蚊帐 是这玩偶的衣裳
这玩偶的眼睛
　　比万物安宁

这玩偶的梦
　飘向我的世界
我的梦多么心酸
夜夜梦见你站在床前
你的手像一把剪刀
时时要把我伤害？

DOLL

Weary of the black night
I often emerge from a dream to sit upright   open my mouth and speak
Little doll gleaming brown
I talk   but the words aren't making sense
I say the crazy things I've always wanted to say

Like a still life   like a lightbulb in the dark
This ugly doll isn't in a hurry
Its inner wildness undetectable
When I switch on the table lamp   dreams kindle on paper
My dreams are sad   I miss my childhood friends
It lies in my hand   and one stab at a time
I stitch on its face and its smile

I dream of the night   it opens its mouth and speaks
Approaches my bedside
The white bed   divided into the realms of yin and yang
The white mosquito net   is the doll's clothing
The eyes of this doll
        Are calmer than all of creation

The dreams of this doll
        Float towards my world
My dreams bring me only heartache
Night after night I see you standing by my bed
Your hand like a pair of scissors
Have you always wanted to hurt me?

肖像

一

你一向拘谨的微笑已杳
但又改换方式　使别人不自觉的眼光
再次领受欺骗
我们都想错了，水只是因为习惯
才慢慢流成某个东西的形状

你从不计算，比许多人更宽容
毁灭性的眼睛将完成你的代表作
秋天享受你时感到不安
太阳发亮，是因为自己内部的原因
不是因为你　你只会爱
却不会被爱

I

Your ever-guarded smile is more distant than ever
but it's changed its look once more   The unsuspecting gazes of others
fall prey to another lie
We were all mistaken, it's only out of habit that water
gradually flows into the shapes it assumes

Never calculating, you're more tolerant than most
Your destructive eyes will put the final touches on this typical work
Autumn enjoys your fits of unease
The sun shines for reasons of its own
and not because of you   You can only love
and never be loved in return

身体

四

在我们丰富的身上
有一个危险附体
巨大的岩石形成雪山的神经
是否比雪还要轻的危险
落在脚下　变成土地？
夏天的黝黑和冬天的白净
全都形神兼备　羽毛一样轻盈
罕见的事物——我们美丽的身体
何时吐蕊？何时飘落？
灵魂末端的花朵在哭泣
衰老飘忽不定的走来
象镜子考验我的耐心

BODY

4

Our rich and fertile bodies
Are possessed by dangerous spirits
Immense boulders from the souls of snowy peaks
Is it a peril even lighter than snow
Falling at our feet   turning into earth?
Summer tan and winter pallor
Body and spirit conjoined   as light as feathers
So rare a sight — our beautiful bodies
When will they flower? When will they fade?
At a loss, blossoms weep
Old age approaches fitfully
Like a mirror appraising my patience

十四首素歌

——致母亲

1　失眠之歌

在一个失眠的夜晚
在许多个失眠的夜晚
我听见失眠的母亲
在隔壁灶旁忙碌
在天亮前浆洗衣物

盲目地在黑暗中回忆过去
它庞大的体积　它不可捉摸的
意义：它凝视将来

那是我们的秘密
不成文的律条
在失眠时　黑夜的心跳
成为我们之间的歌唱：
它凝视将来

盲目地回忆过去
整整一夜我都在猜想
母亲当年的美貌：
她洁白的双颊
纤细的长眼形
从泛黄的相簿里浮起
还有时代的热血
鹰一样锐利的表情
就这样　她戎装成婚
身边　站着瘦削的父亲

FOURTEEN PLAINSONGS

—for my mother

    1 *Insomniac Song*

On a sleepless night
on so many sleepless nights
I hear my restless mother
busy at the stove in the next room
washing clothes before dawn

In the dark thinking of the past
its immense bulk   its unmeasurable
significance: it stares into the future

That's our secret
an unwritten rule
When we can't sleep   the pulse of the black night
is the rhythm of the song we share
It stares into the future

Thinking of the past blindly
I spend the night imagining
my mother's beautiful young face:
her white cheeks
her long and narrow eyes
float up from the yellowed album
The passions of that era
her expression as keen as an eagle's
She was married   in military uniform
my skinny father   at her side

在失眠之夜　母亲灶前灶后
布置一家的生活场景
她是否回忆起那北方的纺锤——
她童年的玩伴？
永远不变的事物使它旋转
就像群星的旋转
它总要围绕一个生命的轴点

多年来我不断失眠
我的失眠总围绕一个轴点：
我凝视母亲

2

低头听见：地底深处
骨头与骨头的交谈
还有闪烁的眼睛奔忙
就如泥土的灵魂
在任何一种黑暗中
听见白昼时：
雄鸡频频啄食　旁若无人

3　黄河谣

母亲说："在那黄河边上
在河湾以南，在新种的小麦地旁
在路的尽端，是我们村"

在黄河岸边　是谢庄
母亲姓谢　名讳

On sleepless nights   mother moves around the stove
arranging the family's life
does she remember that North China spindle ——
her childhood playmate?
Immutable forces make it spin
like the revolutions of constellations
forever circling the hub of a life

For years I've had insomnia
my sleeplessness spinning around a hub:
I stare at my mother

2

Head bowed, I listen deep underground
bones are talking with other bones
glittering eyes dart around
like the spirits of the soil
listening to daylight
from any dark place:
a rooster pecking at grain   as if it were alone

3   *Yellow River Ballad*

Mother says: "On the banks of the Yellow River
south of the Bend, by a plot of newly planted wheat,
at the end of the road, is our village"

On the south side of the Yellow River is Xie village
My mother's family name was Xie   her given name taboo

若香草和美人之称
她从坡脊走来

河流扩大
坡地不断坍塌　泥土
涌到对面的河滩之上
母亲说："我们的地在一点点失去"

于是就有了械斗、迁徙
就有了月黑风高时的抢劫
一个鬼魂的泅渡
就有了无数鬼魂的奢望
那些韶华红颜的年轻女孩
他们的爱人都已逝去
"在黄河上刮来的刮去的寒风
每年刮着他们年轻的尸骨"

虽然河水枯黄、石滩粗糙
但母亲出落得动人
她的脸像杏子
血色像桃花
当她走过坡脊
她是黄河边上最可爱的事物
当她在河边赤脚踩踏衣服
一股寒意刺痛了岸边的小伙
使他们的内心一阵阵懊恼

我的四十岁比母亲来得更早
像鸟儿一只只飞走
那一年年熟视无睹的时间
我天生的忧伤锁在骨髓里
不被走在我身旁的人所察觉
我的四十岁比母亲来得更早

Like an ancient hero pure of heart
she walked down from the ridge

The river is broad
its banks forever collapsing   and mud
washes up on the opposite shore
Mother says: "Our land was disappearing"

So people clashed, or moved away
There was looting on moonless nights
One ghost swam across the river
and countless others were filled with wild hopes
The girls were blossoming
but their lovers were dead
"The freezing winds that blow back and forth across the Yellow River
stream over their young bones"

Though the river ran the ochre of drought, and the shingled shoreline
                    was rugged
my mother was stunningly beautiful
her face like an apricot
rosy as peach blossoms
When she strode along the ridge
she was the prettiest girl by the Yellow River
When she walked barefoot on its banks, stepping on the washing
the young men felt an icy stab
and shuddered with regret

My forty years went by more quickly than my mother's
one by one, they flew away like birds
Year after year, time passed by, unremarkable
an inborn sadness locked inside my marrow
and those who walked beside me never noticed
My forty years went by more quickly than my mother's

"什么样的男人是我们的将来？
什么样的男人使我们等到迟暮？
什么样的男人在我们得到时
与失去一样悲痛？
什么样的男人
与我们的睡眠和死亡为伴？"

我的母亲从坡脊上走来
挟着书包　还没有学会
一种适合她终身的爱　但
已经知道作女人的弊病
和恋爱中那些可耻的事情
她没有丝绸　身着麻布衣衫
谁看见她
谁就会忘记自己的一切

使遥远的事物变得悲哀
使美变得不朽
时间的笔在急速滑动
产生字　就像那急速滑落的河滩上
倾泄如注的卵
不顾及新坟中死亡者的痛苦
流到东　流到南
又拍打到对面
不顾及人们为它死在两岸

4

事物都会凋零
时间是高手　将其施舍
充作血肉的营养
精液流出它们自己的空间
包括临终时最后的一点

"What kind of man is our future?
What kind of man makes us wait till the twilight of our years?
What kind of man makes getting him
as painful as losing him?
What kind of man
will lie beside us in sleep and death?"

My mother walks along the ridge
book bag under her arm   She still hasn't learned the ways of
a love worth keeping till the end of her days
She already knows the pitfalls of being a woman
and the shameful things that go with love
She has no silks   she's dressed in hemp
Whoever sees her
will lose himself completely

Turning faraway events into tragedies
making beauty everlasting
the brush of time glides rapidly along
giving birth to words   like pebbles pouring down
rapidly sliding banks
careless of the suffering dead in fresh graves
Flowing east   flowing south
slapping the opposite shore
careless of the people who died for it on either side

    4

Everything withers in the end
Time has the upper hand   when giving out alms
to sustain the flesh
Semen flows from every cavity
right until the last drop at the hour of death

5 十八岁之歌

母亲说：在她的少女时代
风暴和斗争来到她的身边
钢枪牵起了她的手
尸骸遍野塞满了她的眼睛

我的母亲：儿童团长
她的兄长挎枪乘马
是远近驰名的勇士
生生死死
不过如闺房中的游戏　她说
她放下织梭
跟着爱人远去

敌人来到：携枪、或运炮
村庄被倾覆　亲戚四散奔逃
在母亲的眼里　我看到
那些人的影象：
他们是我的姑表中亲
血缘里的一部分
有时从相册里探出没有呼吸的脸
或者目光严峻
或者沉默寡言
战斗、献身、矢志不移
他们被血浸透的单纯
像火一样点燃　在那些战争年代

我的十八岁无关紧要
我的十八岁开不出花来
与天空比美　但
我的身体里一束束的神经
能感觉到植物一批批落下

5   The Song of Being Eighteen

Mother said: when she was young
Strife and turmoil found her
A rifle in her hands
corpse-covered fields filling her vision

My mother: leader of a children's brigade
Her commander rode on horseback, shouldering a gun
a man renowned for his courage
Life and death
were like boudoir games   she said
She set aside her shuttle
and followed her lover far away

The enemy arrived pointing guns and firing cannons
The village was in chaos   kinsmen scattered to the four winds
In mother's eyes I saw
images of these people:
cousins and aunts
a branch of my bloodline
I turn to a lifeless face in the album
Some stare out sternly
some are tight-lipped and glum
Warfare, sacrifice, unwavering dedication
their purity drenched in blood
blazed like fire through years of war

My eighteenth year brought nothing of note
My eighteenth year bore no flowers
Beautiful as the sky   and yet
every sheaf of nerves in my body
could feel plants withering clump by clump

鸟儿在一只只死去　我身内的
各种花朵在黑夜里左冲右突
撞在前前后后的枯骨上
我的十八岁无关紧要

在那些战争年代　我的母亲
每天在生的瞬间和死的瞬间中
穿行　她的美貌和
她双颊的桃花点染出
战争最诡奇的图案
她秀发剪短　步履矫健
躲避着丛林中的枪子和
敌人手中的导火线　然后
她积极的身躯跑向
另一个爆破点

母亲讲述的故事
都有大胆的结论
不寻常的死亡方式——牺牲
或不具体的
更悲切的动机　不同于我
对死亡的担心
对虚无世界的忧心忡忡
对已经到来　将要离去的
归宿的疑问

没有人来听我们的演说
也没有人关心我们相互的存在
当然　也没有人来追捕我们
亡命的生涯　而且
也没有子弹穿过
我们的鬓发　没有五星
成为我的发饰　我只是

birds dying one by one   The riot of flowers
inside my body exploded under cover of darkness
crashing into the dry bones surrounding them
My eighteenth year brought nothing of note

In those years of war   my mother
threaded through the space between the instants
of life and death   Her fair features and
rosy cheeks colored
the strangest gambit of the war
She cut off her glossy hair   striding purposefully
eluding guns in the woods and
fuses held in the enemy's hands   and then
she hurled her body full tilt
towards yet another blast

All the stories mother told
had rousing conclusions
and extraordinary deaths —— sacrifice
or an abstract
and even sadder impulse   unlike me with my
fretting about death
my anxiousness about this false and empty world
and my long present   but soon to depart
misgivings about going home

No one comes to hear our speeches
No one cares that we're here
Of course   no one is chasing us down
in a world of mortal prospects   What's more
no bullets are whistling past
our ears   I don't have five stars
to pin in my hair   I've merely

让幻想穿透我的身体
让一个命运的逆转成为我
骨髓里的思想

6

——"**最终，我们无法忍受**"
黑眼女子端坐火边
中立的发型前趋
离别像一把刀 等待
男人的心入鞘
而女人掌握了使它流血的技巧

7　建设之歌

我的出生地：
一座寺庙　几间危房
高处一座黑塔
护卫我的：一个本地女孩
战争搞乱了母亲们的生育
胎儿如幽灵向外张望　但
没有权利选择时间
如果能够选择
我该会选择第一个出生
而不是最后　如果
选择能够改变人类的第一步
我将躲开各种各样的命运
或者最好的一种
或者早夭

let my body be shot through with illusions
and allowed a twist of fate to become
the ideology in my bones

6

——"In the end, we couldn't bear it"
A dark-eyed woman sitting tall beside the fire
she'd charged forward with her unisex haircut
Separation like a knife   poised
A man's heart slides into its sheath
but a woman holds it tight until she bleeds

7   *The Song of Reconstruction*

My birthplace:
a temple   a few crumbling rooms
high up in a black pagoda
My protector: a local girl
War had wreaked havoc on many mothers' labors
Fetuses looked out on the world like ghosts   and yet
we lacked the power to choose our time
Had there been a choice
I would have been the first born
rather than the last   and if
choice could alter a human being's first step
I could have evaded all manner of fates
whether one of the best
or an early death

事实上　我出生：
向着任意的方向
来不及分析哪样更好？
在母体的小小黑暗里
还是在世界广大的白昼中

万物像江河奔来
像阳光刺痛我的双眼
接连几个月　我紧闭两眼
躺在床上　那是我
终身要躺的地方

我的母亲　戎装在身
红旗和歌潮如海地
为她添妆
而我　则要等到多年后
在另一个狂欢的时代
模仿母亲的着装
好似去参加一个化装舞会

"我们是创建者"　母亲说
她的理想似乎比生命本身
更重要　创建是快乐的
比之于毁坏
人们懂得这一点

铁锤敲击蓝图
现代之城在建设的高音区
普遍地成长
高大、雄伟、有谁在乎
匍匐在它脚下的时间之城
那有争议的美

In reality   I was born
with a stubborn streak
Would I fail to perceive what was best:
staying inside the cramped darkness of my mother's body
or being out in the expansive daylight of the world?

All of creation rushes in like a river
stabbing my eyes like sunlight
For several months in a row   I've kept my eyes shut tight
lying on my bed   That's where I'll be
lying 'til the end of my days

My mother   in uniform
red flags and songs, a rising tide,
adorned her
but I   would wait for years
for another ecstatic era
copying my mother's way of dressing
as if I were going to a costume party

"We were founders"   Mother said
Her ideals seemed more important
than life itself   Founding is joyful
compared to destruction
That's something anyone can understand

Hammers strike blueprints
A modern city in the high pitch of reconstruction
grows up around us
Immense, imposing, and who will spare a thought for
the historic city lying prostrate at its feet
That's the beauty of conflict

为建设奔忙的母亲
肉体的美一点点的消散
而时间更深邃的部分
显出它永恒不变的力量

8

没有一个男人回头望
他们爬出针眼
注视敌人的眼睛
在交媾时威风八面
直到在寒冷中下葬

9　观察蚂蚁的女孩之歌

蚂蚁移动着　来回穿梭
像移动一个纯净的下午
一个接一个　排列成行
偶然相互拥抱

"我听见你们在说话"
观察蚂蚁的女孩　我说

她出现了　在周围极端的小中
她是那样大　真正的大
她有自己的冠冕
蚁王有她自己的风范

"我用整个的身体倾听
内心的天线在无限伸展

Mother busy with nation-building
her sensual beauty rubbed away bit by bit
and an even more profound place in time
reveals an immutable power

8

Not one man looks back
They crawl out of the needle's eye
staring down the enemy
engaging in dignified sex
until they're laid to rest in the wintry cold

9   *The Song of the Girl Who Observes the Ants*

Ants are milling around   shuttling back and forth
as if moving a chaste afternoon
one after another   lined up single file
sometimes embracing

"I heard you talking among yourselves"
the girl who observes the ants   I say

She appeared   surrounded by such minuteness
She was that large   genuinely large
She had a crown of her own
The queen ant had her own kind of style

"I listened with my entire body
my inner antennae extending their infinite reach

我嗅到风、蜜糖天气
和一个静态世界里的话语"
——观察蚂蚁的女孩 "是我"
蚂蚁溢满了我的火柴盒
它所在的世界没有风
没有话语 它们
轻轻一触目 触摸到什么？
从那不可见的事物中
得到我们不可见的消息

这时 我突然置身在
那巨大的火柴盒里 她那
巨大的冠冕 残忍地盖住我
她那巨大的呼吸和叹气
吹动我的命运 我的身体
她在一个女孩眼中的形体
和火柴盒在她眼中的形体
是这个世界的变异

"妈妈，请给我一个火柴盒"
观察蚂蚁的女孩 我说

10

一切都无忧无虑
——老人低头弈棋
调整呼吸 不考虑身前身后
急如旋风的纪念
他的枯干骨指老而益尖

I smelled the wind, the nectared weather
and the speech of a world at peace"
—— the girl who observes the ants   "It's me"
Ants overflow my matchbox
living in a world without wind
without speech   When they
gently catch your eye   what is being caught?
From within something invisible
we gather invisible news

And then   I'm suddenly inside
a gigantic matchbox   That giant
crown of hers   covers me without pity
Her enormous breaths and sighs
buffet my fate   My body
her form in a young girl's eyes
and the form of the matchbox in her eyes
embody the mutability of this world

"Mama, please give me a matchbox"
the girl who observes the ants   I say

10

Freed from care and released from woe
—— an old man bends over a game of Go
regulates his breathing   thinking neither of the past nor the hereafter
memories sudden as whirlwinds
his withered and boney fingers grown sharper with age

11 舞蹈的女人之歌

母亲说：你本名萍
萍踪何处？萍影漂泊
神秘的镜子里我笑不出

我、家族的下一代
经过一个肃杀的童年
和一个苦恼的少年
现在进入寂寞的时代
我的三十岁马马虎虎

诱惑我的感情已不重要
"当爱来临，将取走你的眼睛"
桌边：一杯劣质咖啡
一下午的偎颈共语
一个被称为柏拉图式的爱情
毁了我的青春

我的母亲不相信她的亲眼所见
还有那些白发长者：
在月光下　在临水的河边
我全身抽搐　如吐火女怪
鬼似的起舞　骨骼发出吓人的声响
我当众摇摆的形体
使她憎恶

我就地燃烧的身体
让他们目瞪口呆
他们不明白为什么
肉体的美会如此颤抖
连同肉体的羞耻
他们习惯于那献身的
信仰的旋律

11　The Song of the Dancing Woman

Mother said: I named you "Ping," rootless duckweed
where do you wander? Duckweed, drifting on the water
I can't conjure a smile in that mysterious mirror

I, the next generation of my family
had a cold and lonely childhood
a difficult adolescence
Now I'm entering an age of solitude
My thirtieth year was just so-so

Feelings that once seduced me no longer matter
"When love comes calling, turn your eyes away"
At the table: a cup of bad coffee
An afternoon of whispering and touching
A love we called Platonic
destroyed my youth

My mother couldn't believe what she saw
not to mention the white-haired elders:
In the moonlight　　　　by the riverbank
my body shaking all over　　　like a she-monster spewing fire
I began a ghoulish dance　　　bones making a horrible sound
My form swaying there for all to see
filled her with loathing

My body blazed before them
left them glassy-eyed and dumbstruck
unable to comprehend how
the beauty of the flesh could shudder
along with the shame of the flesh
accustomed as they were to self-sacrifice
and zealous melodies

于是　舞蹈从中心散尽
带着母亲的斥责四处逃掉
还有我那些不明真相的同类
风　把他们各自的骚乱送得很远
我的二十岁马马虎虎

如今漂泊日久　劳作多年
与另一名男子爱欲如狂
我终于到达一个和谐　与青春
与一个不再残酷的舞蹈

12

因此在一夜间
被美逼近
在一绺发丝缠绕下
爱和恨　改弦易辙
培育出幻影
并随青春的酒浆
恸哭或销魂

13　黑白的片断之歌

现在　我敲打我那黑白的
打字机键盘
颇为自得
像干一件蠢事般自得

我已不再用自己的心灵思索？
那一大堆字母

And so   the dance is flung from the center
carrying mother's rebuke to the ends of the earth
There are people like me who don't see things as they are
The wind   takes each one's miseries far far away
My twentieth year was just so-so

I've been drifting so long   toiling for years
am madly in love with yet another man
At last I've made my peace   with youth
with a dance that won't be cruel again

12

And so in one night
pressed by beauty
beneath a winding tendril of hair
love and hate change their tunes
fostering an illusion
trying to keep up with the elixir of youth
crying out in pain or melting with joy

13   *The Song of Black and White Paragraphs*

Now I strike my black and white
keyboard
pleased with myself
pleased with myself though it might seem stupid

Can't I think for myself anymore?
A bunch of letters of the alphabet

组合成的五笔字形？
像水草　在一片蓝色中流动
能否流出事物的本来面目
它不知道一级解码的过程
它呈现：就是终极的面目

我的四十岁比母亲来得早
骨髓里的忧伤是她造成的
她不知道　但她的思想
暗暗散发进我的体内　就像
一盘桃子的芳香暗暗
散发进我的鼻孔　她造成
我倦怠生命中最深远的痕迹
比任何黑白字母的渗透更有力
我的四十岁比母亲来得更早

当我敲打我那黑白的
打字机键盘　用肘紧靠桌面
母亲弯腰坐在她的缝纫机旁
用肘支撑衰老
敲打她越来越简单的生活
从她的姿势
到我的姿势
有一点从未改变：
那凄凉的、最终的
纯粹的姿势
不是以理念为投影
在我体内有一点血脉
稠密的一点
来自母亲的容颜
她那桃花式的血色素
我未能继承
成为生命里部分的遗憾

Big Five text?
Like marsh grasses   waving in a blue expanse
can they flow from the original face of things
not knowing the first stage of decoding
they appear: the final look of things

My fortieth year arrived more quickly than my mother's
The wounds in my marrow were of her making
She didn't know   but still her thinking
spread through my body in secret   the way
the scent of peaches in a bowl subtly
fans out and enters my nose   She left
the most profound mark on my exhausted existence
deeper and wider than any black and white letters
My fortieth year arrived more quickly than my mother's

While I strike my black and white
keyboard   elbows pressed to my desk
Mother sits over her sewing machine
elbows propping up her frailty
striking her ever simplifying life   .
From her gesture
to my gesture
one thing has never changed:
that desolate and final
pure gesture
not the projection of an idea
There's a tiny blood vessel in me
a dense little spot
that came from my mother's face
a peach-like rosy pigment
I couldn't inherit
the regret that became a part of life

除此之外　我继承着：
黄河岸边的血肉
十里枯滩的骨头
水边的尘沙
云上的日子
来自男方的模子和
来自女方的脾性
还有那四十岁就已来到的
衰老　它重叠：
就是终极的面目

始于那坍塌的坡地
和一点点移向他方的泥土
堆积起来的村庄的意志
终于一种不变的变化
缓慢地，靠近时间本质
在我们双肘确立的地方

14

于是谈到诗时　　不再动摇：
——就如推动冰块
在酒杯四壁赤脚跳跃
就如铙钹撞击它自己的两面
伤害　　玻璃般的痛苦——
词、花容、和走投无路的爱

Other than that   I did inherit:
flesh and blood from the Yellow River's banks
bones from ten miles of barren strands
dust from the water's edge
days from above the clouds
my build from the male side and
my temperament from the female
Reaching the age of forty
old and worn   it piles up:
the final look of things

Beginning with those collapsing banks
a village's mounting ambitions
the mud shifting elsewhere bit by bit
In the end, an immutable mutability
gradually nears the essence of time
where our elbows are firmly braced

14

So when we speak of poetry   we no longer waver:
—— it's like stirring ice cubes
it's like pairs of cymbals crashing into each other's faces
Wounded   suffering like glass ——
words, fair faces, and love at an impasse

剪刀手的对话

一

"对我说吧，僵硬的逃亡"
一根脉络和无数枝叶移动
围绕肝脏 本能地摇摆

"对我说吧，耐心点"
献给卡洛的长形剪刀
导致我肺部的感染

蝴蝶一扑 点燃她满嘴的桃红
女人的颜色来自痛
痉挛、和狂怒

"对我说吧，僵硬的剪刀手
我不会躺在七零八落的敲打中
让那年迈医生的钢针
和他考察病理的目光
为我如此妆扮"

"捣碎的脊柱，不如一根铁钉
我已得到足够的治疗"

二

俯身向玻璃 剃刀边缘
察看毛孔的健康状况
和受伤的皮囊
我，游离在五光十色之间
深入…浅出…
"为了美，女人永远着忙"

SCISSORHANDS' DIALOGUE

For Frida Kahlo

1

"Tell me about it, the rigid escape"
A vein and many branches and leaves aflutter
Encircling viscera   swaying by instinct

"Tell me, but be patient"
Long-bladed shears offered up to Kahlo
Bring infection to my lungs

A butterfly beats its wings   igniting the rosy red of her lips
Women's colors come from pain
Convulsions and rage

"Tell me, rigid scissor hands
I can't lie down in the middle of this random pounding
To let that elderly doctor's steel needle
And his diagnostic gaze
Primp and dress me up like that"

"Pulverized vertebrae, I opted for an iron rod,
I got the cure I needed"

2

I lean over the glass   a razor's edge
Examining my pores
And this damaged bag of bones
Me, roaming among the colors of the rainbow
Entering the depths . . . surfacing in the shallows
"Women will always go to great lengths for beauty"

请看体内的锻铁钉
在一朵忧郁烈焰的炙烤下
斑斓 怎样变成她胸前的雕花图案

洗涤槽中，血水
与口红的色彩波动
冰冷的上方
我那眩晕的兜售者
从红肿的双眼里
喷出瀑布 蔑视感染

"玻璃或钻石
还有撩拨人的目光
促使她疯狂"

三

蜂鸟，刺藤的拥抱
掠过她狂热的
流血的脖子 创造美的脸庞

蝴蝶一扑 飞起来
从卡洛冰凉的铁床上
闪光、金黄
吱吱响的四只车轮
目睹了这个女人的战场

一根根向上长的毛发
和她的浓眉是
内心茂盛繁荣的气象
穿透石膏护身褡
穿透塌下来的一片天

Look at the iron rod inside my body
Beneath a bloom of sad and angry flames
How were those rainbow hues transformed   into the patterns
              carved on her breast

In the basin bloody water
Ripples with lipstick colors
Icy destiny
Me, the dizzy hawker
Spewing waterfalls
Scorning the contagion   with red and swollen eyes

"Glass and diamonds
Both catch the eye with their allure
Spurring women to madness"

      3

Hummingbird, embraced by thorny vines
Brushing past her fevered
Bleeding neck   creating a beautiful face

Butterfly beats its wings   flutters up
From Kahlo's ice-cold metal bed
Flashing, golden
Four wheels creaking
Witness to this woman's battlefield

Each and every living hair and
Her heavy eyebrows
Are the fertile climate of her heart
Piercing the plaster cast
Piercing the collapsing sky

"我己掌握了恐惧的形状"
卡洛俯身向前，低声细语
我听见剪刀轧轧之响
以及石膏、拐杖
它们痛断肝肠

####### 四

剃刀边缘　闪着钻石的光
成为我前胸主动的安排
发式在意念中变幻　忽长忽短
暗夜的香味浆洗着双眼

双眼　越靠近玻璃面　越黑
她的呕吐打击著盘旋的光线
令人担忧：欢乐的背面

背面：你来看
浓浓淡淡　黑白的光影
一株植物从最多减到单一
她洗净颜色……
何如一杯在手

"为了美，女人暗暗淌血"

淌血　谁会在乎：
她心中的剪刀正在剪
一个爱的真轮廓　她注视
动物之眼一样犀利
两腿绞动着　发出嘶嘶声

"I have grasped the shape of terror"
Kahlo leans forward, whispering
I hear the scissors slicing
Plaster, and cane
They're broken hearted

4

Razor's edge   flashing diamantine lights
Become a moving pattern on my breast
Hairstyles leave dreamlike memories   now long, now short
The dark night's fragrance washes over my eyes until they gleam

A pair of eyes   the closer they get to the glass   the darker they grow
Her vomit strikes spinning beams of light
Making me sad: the other side of joy

The other side: come see
The dense and the thin   the black and white of light and shadow
Plants decreasing from multitudes to just one
She's rinsed clean of color . . .
Why not pick up a glass

"For beauty, women bleed in secret"

They bleed but who cares:
The scissors in her heart are cutting
Love's true outlines   she stares
Eyes sharp as an animal's
Two legs scissoring   hissing, hissing

嘶嘶　盐一样刺痛的声音
它不是从口中呜咽
也不是在耳边温柔
它是一根舌头绞动无望的花茎

五

在黑暗中　我的腿脚伸出
与卡洛跳舞
"女人们：来，去
蜡烛般烧毁自己的本性"

"不必管那眼神够得着的搜寻
卡洛，我们破碎的脊柱
服从内心性欲的主动"

年幼者取悦漂亮的玻璃
为毁灭的碎片受苦
年长者沉默不语
像竖强有力的石头的灵魂
着魔时，也保持内部的完好无损

"为了美，女人痛断肝肠"

双腿绞动着　剪刀手
修剪黑暗的形状
忙着切开、砍、分割
忙着消毒、闪光
何人如此适合
握住道把手术刀　挂满高嘲笑
要对付我们共同的腰病
卡洛——我们怎样区分来自剪刀刀锋
或是来自骨髓深处的痛？

Hissing   as prickly as salt
It's not a moan
It's not easy on the ear
It's the hopeless and tangled pistil of the tongue

    5

In the darkness   my legs extended
Dancing with Kahlo
"Women: coming and going
Burning away your essence like candles"

"Don't pay attention to what meets the eye
Kahlo, our broken spines
Obey the desiring heart and its urgings"

The young find pleasure in the pretty pieces of glass
While the old subside into silence
Suffering for shattered fragments
Like the spirits of strong and faithful stones
Spellbound, they remain whole within

"For beauty, women will suffer heartbreak"

A pair of legs crossing   scissorhands
Snipping away at shapes in the darkness
Busily chopping, cutting, splitting
Busily disinfecting, glinting
Who could be better at
Wielding this scalpel   and sneering
At our common spinal malady
Kahlo — how can we know if the source of our pain is the scissors' tip
Or the depths of our own marrow?

盲人按摩师的几种方式

1

"请把手放下"，盲人俯身
推拿腰部，也像推拿石头
生活的腰多么空虚
引起疼痛

盲人一天又一天推拿按摩
推拿比石头还硬的腰部

2

"注意气候，气候改变一切，"
梅花针执在盲人之手
我尽力晃动头部："这是什么？"

生命，是易碎的事物
还是骨头，骨节，骨密度？
梅花针扎在我的头部

3

"请敲骨椎第一节，那里疼痛"
盲人的手按下旋律的白键
"这声音怎么这样凄凉？"

我知道疼痛的原因
是生命的本质，与推拿无关
但推拿已进入和谐的境界
盲人一天又一天敲打
分享我骨头里的节奏

THE BLIND MASSEUR AND SOME OF HIS METHODS

1

"Relax your hands," the blind man leans over
Kneading the small of my back, as if he were kneading stone
The waist of life is so empty
It hurts

Day after day the blind man massages
Kneading backs that are harder than stone

2

"Be mindful of the climate, climate changes everything,"
Plum blossom needle held in the blind man's hand
I strain to move my head: "What is that?"

Is it life that's fragile
Or is it bones, joints, and bone density?
Plum blossom needles stab my head

3

"Please tap my first vertebra, it's sore"
The blind man's hand plays out a melody on white keys
"Why does it sound so sad?"

I know where the pain comes from
It's the nature of life itself, and nothing to do with this massage
But the massage has reached a state of harmony
The blind man taps, day after day
Sharing in the rhythms of my bones

4

"转过身去，调匀呼吸"
盲人的手按下旋律的黑键

暴风雨般的即兴弹奏
他空洞的眼里无怨无欲
甚至他的呼吸也极度平静
他的两手推拿世间的问题
盲人有盲人的方式

他思索下手的轻重缓急
与我们的方向一致

5

"请注意骶骨的变化"，他说
他的手指熟知全世界的穴位
他的手掌兼修中西两种功力

当他使劲，十根指头落下
贯注全身的一股深邃力量知道
一种痛苦已被摧毁

另一种痛苦来自肺腑
来自白色袍子的适当切入
以及我那怯懦的心跳

6

盲人一天又一天摸索
熟悉的事物，渐渐地
渐渐地达到澄明的高度

4

"Turn over, breathe evenly"
The blind man's hands play a melody on black keys

A stormy solo improvisation
His vacant eyes are without complaint or desire
Even his breathing is unusually calm
His hands massage the problems of the world
The blind man works in a blind man's ways

He thinks about the lightness and speed of his touch
As we face the same direction

5

"Pay attention to changes in your sacrum," he says
His fingers know the world's accupressure points by heart
His palms are practiced in Eastern and Western ways

When he applies force, ten fingers press down
The profound strength of his whole body concentrated here and knowing
One kind of pain has already been erased

Another kind of pain comes from deep in my heart
From the suitable cut of the white gown
And my tentative pulse

6

The blind man feels his way, day after day
Familiar things, bit by bit
Bit by bit achieving complete clarity

从一块坚硬的石头，或者
在空气中飞舞的跳动的尘埃

一男一女，两个盲人
看不见变易中的生死
看得见生死中的各种变易

7

一次，他拿出两个罐子
其中一个是空的，另一个也空

一滴水就从身体里慢慢溢出
但是他看不见，现在他抽掉
里面的空气，点燃酒精棉
他想要得到什么？

除了腰椎的十四个关节
还有骨头深处的阵阵寒意……

8

响了一夜的孤寂之声
"现在好了，寒气已经散尽"
他收起罐子，万物皆有神力
那铿锵的滴水的音律
我知道和所有的骨头有关

一天又一天雨下个不停
盲人按摩师的手抓住的
是不是那石头般的内心恐惧？

From a rigid piece of stone, or
A dust mote dancing in the air

A man and a woman, both of them blind
Unable to see Life and Death amidst all the changes
Able to see the transformations within Life and Death

7

Once, he takes out a pair of jars
The first of them empty, the other one empty as well

A bead of water oozes slowly from my body
But he can't see it, and then he draws out
The air inside, lights a piece of alcohol-soaked cotton
What is he trying to achieve?

Apart from my fourteen lumbar vertebrae
There are tremors of cold deep in my bones . . .

8

A lone voice
"It's better now, the cold energy has been dissipated"
He puts away the jars, all of creation has extraordinary power
I know the ringing tones of the water drop
Are linked to all of my bones

Day after day, the rain falls incessantly
What do the hands of the blind masseur grasp
Is it a stony and deep seated fear?

9

"这里怎样？这里应该是
感官的触动，这条肌肉
和骨头之间有一种痛
能触动你的神经，压迫
你的手臂，毁灭你的黑夜

不要让风穿过你的身体
不要让恐惧改变你。"

10

如果能把痛楚化成
有形的东西，类似
抓住一把盐，洒在地上

类似端走一盆清水
从皮肤里，类似
擦掉苹果上的污迹

类似手指按下琴键
随即又轻轻地移开

11

手指间的舞蹈，很轻
指力却浑厚，生命中的
强弱之音此时都在

盲人坐着，细说记忆
那触手一摸，心灵的辨识
比眼睛的触摸更真实

"How does it feel right here? This spot should
Trigger your senses, between this strip of muscle
And bone there is a tenderness
That can touch your nerves, restrict
Your arms, blot out your dark nights

Don't let any drafts penetrate your body
Don't let yourself be altered by fear."

10

If pain could be transformed
Into something that had a shape, like
Grabbing a handful of salt, scattering it on the ground

Like carrying away a basin of clear water
From inside the skin, like
Wiping dirt from an apple

Like fingers striking the keys of a piano
Then moving lightly away

11

The dance between fingers, so light
While the fingers' strength is solid, the powerful and weak
Sounds of Life are all here in this moment

The blind man sits, sharing his memories
When you touch something with your hands, what the spirit perceives
Is truer than what meets the eyes

大脑中反复重叠的事物
比看得见的一切更久长

12

尘世中的一大堆杂念
被你熔与黑暗一炉
终将打成整铁一片

当你想看，你就能看
最终达于静止的世界
日子年复一年，并不休息

盲人俯身，推拿
疼痛的中心，一天又一天

The accumulated things that fill your mind
Are more enduring than all that you see

12

A mass of jumbled thoughts in this material world
Melted by you in the furnace of darkness
Struck at last into one great sheet of iron

When you're ready to see, you'll be able to see
A world that has achieved tranquility
The days go by, year after year, without rest

The blind man leans over, massaging
The center of the pain, day after day

更衣室

四个墙角 蹲着四角布帘
款款开衩的裙衫
随同它们的鱼尾摆
我的更衣室 层层叠叠
坐着小玩偶 它们
易碎的瞳孔狂暴地
揪住金鱼缸   瞧
我走来 紫水晶抱住一团风
那才是别样的肌

百变的古典长裙呵护我的
神情冷落   别样的骨瘦如柴
在这四角 贪食的女人吞掉
肮脏的色彩 吞掉成吨的液体
它们是女人的月全蚀
让我抬起头来 (沧桑
脆弱的额头) 更衣室为我
付出甚么 让我们排队
如同排队上天堂

不变的红色连衣裙
女友为我披上 一身如血的
狂舞之妆
女友的黑色褶皱衫
把暴戾藏于哭泣的方式中
还好 针尖、绑带和一些玉石
像母爱的避邪之物 贴住
永不过时的迷信一族
还好 我们蜘蛛般爬满
印花布帘 我们有了用途
在更衣室 妆成大胆的图案

THE CHANGING ROOM

Four corners   passing time inside four curtained corners
flowing dresses slit so high
their fish tails swishing side to side
My changing room   tier after tier of
little dolls ensconced   their
fragile pupils violently
fasten onto the goldfish bowl   catch
me strolling by   amethyst crystals embrace the draft
another kind of skin

Ever-changing old-fashioned dress, how it guards my
chilly hauteur   I'm thin as kindling
In these four corners   hungry women gorge on
soiled colors   gulping down gallons of liquid
a woman's full lunar eclipse
Let me lift my head   (Time and tide
ravage these delicate brows)   The changing room gives me
something   has us form a line
as if we were lining up to enter Heaven

Never-changing red dress
a friend slips it onto me   blood red from head to toe
costumed for a mad dance
My friend's black pleated blouse
conceals wracking sobs behind stylized tears
and it's fine   needles, bandages, a few pieces of jade
like talismans blessed with maternal love   attached to
the superstitious ones who never go out of style
It's all right   like a horde of spiders
we cover the printed curtains   we have our uses
in the changing room   dressing up our bold plans

在我小小的更衣室
我变换性别、骨头和发根
沉闷的嗓音在念儿童读物:
"一个冬天的早晨、一场火灾……
奔跑的乙炔扑打风
雪地上的红色伤了我"

我变来变去的注目礼
被万事万物的依旧吃掉
同学们威胁我　那些目光
像一张张嘴的尖叫
在我小小的更衣室
我变换身材、手势和憨笑
听见一个男人在念儿童读物:
"揪心的学校　揪心的
回家的路　母亲站在面前
像橱窗内的礼物……"

换来换去的黑色布鞋
被蚂蚁般增长的时间撑破
午睡时的不眠　换来
一夜间的生长　同学们
看着我　他们破坏性的微笑
让我找不到自救

在我小小的更衣室里
我变换眼波、汗毛和体味
黑暗中有人在念儿童读物:
"哭泣的急救室　火焰的恐惧
植入皮肤　还有收音机的嘶叫
浸进耳膜　这脆若薄纸的幼年……"
变和不变的世界找到我　安慰我
青青校树的生长比我快得多
同学们　围着我

In my little changing room
I change my gender, bones and hair, down to the roots
A listless voice reads a children's book:
"One winter morning, there was a great fire . . .
acetylene racing and slapping the wind
Scarlet on the snow wounded me"

My quicksilver ritualistic eye contact
has been eaten by the habitual universe
My classmates threaten me   their piercing looks
like screeches from each of their mouths
In my little changing room
I alter my figure, my gestures, my vacuous smile
and listen to a man reading a children's book:
"The anxious school   the anxious
road home   My mother standing before me
like a gift in a shop window . . ."

Black cloth shoes changed in and out of
burst open by the long ant trail of Time
Sleeplessness at siesta   exchanged for
a night of growth   My classmates
watch me   their broken smiles
blocking my exits

In my little changing room
I alter my come-hither glances, downy skin and scent
someone is reading a children's book in the dark:
"The weeping emergency room   the terror of flames
takes root in my skin   the shriek of the radio
invades my ears   the paper-thin years of childhood . . ."
The changing yet unchanging world finds me   comforts me
Verdant trees at school grow much faster than I do
My classmates   surround me

他们全体的眼睛　比我的眼睛
大　比我清　以及灿烂

在我小小的更衣室
我变换发式、内衣和血型
我的高音清脆　念着儿童读物：
"伤心的苹果　偷走的童年脸颊
人丛里有一个声音喊：
母亲啊母亲　离别就在眼前"

搬来搬去的家像季节变换
转眼就到了典卖"过去"的日子
同学们离开语法　和捣乱的金属牙套

四个墙角　蹲著四角布帘
它们是空空哀愁制成的材料
注视我的赤裸　腰部的僵硬和
小小玩偶的张口结舌　我可以和
四角玻璃缸里的鱼泡
同时升起　看房子四周那些
已结婚的人　烹调和谈天

看更远处　四方屋檐下
整夜追逐恐惧的灯光
与人形的隔窗之感
我的小小更衣室　当沮丧来临
我在这里睡眠　当有人说我"笨拙"
我在这里睡眠　这些灰绿色的衣衫
这些灰绿色的温柔眼睛　这些灰绿色
软性的东西敷我　绵绵的氤氲
把我和门外隔开　我的隔世之眼
宜深宜远

altogether their eyes   are larger
clearer   brighter   than mine

In my little changing room
I change my hairstyle, lingerie, and blood type
My voice is high and clear   I read a children's story:
"The sorrowful apple   the stolen cheeks of childhood
A voice shouts out from the crowd:
Mother, O Mother   it's time to say goodbye"

The constantly moving household changes like the seasons
Every time you turn around it's time to mortgage "the past"
My classmates abandon grammar   sowing disorder
                    with sets of metal teeth

Four walls and corners   passing time in four curtained corners
all this stuff fashioned from wasted grief
Gazing at my naked back   stiff waist and
the gaping mouths of little dolls   I might
float up with the bubbles in that four-cornered
fish bowl   and watch the married people
within the four walls of this house   the cookery and small talk

Seeing even farther   under the eaves of these four-sided courtyards
searching all night for that frightening lamplight
and a sense of human figures behind the windows
My little changing room   When depression comes to call
this is where I sleep   When people call me "clumsy"
this is where I sleep   these gray-green clothes
these gentle gray-green eyes   these silken gray-green
substances annoint my body   heavy clouds of vapor
cut me off from the outside world   this sleep from another era
**   so distant and deep**

水中的弟弟

水　兼有一室沧浪
　　兼有一点悲伤
凌空倒进体内的香水瓶
我嗅啊嗅
嗅到分别的寒气
座中有我所爱　弟弟
在我的右侧　匆匆改了装
水呀　淹过了脚趾

"我"　回答时像含着一枚果
吐出来像深深的长矛
宝石光样的　孤注一掷
迷失了它的背影
弟弟　当夏日逼人　我愿
绘一张簪花小影
看看我眼里的气　透出纸背
射向云　能否
达到更深的洁癖？
水呀　淹过了脚踵

我们的双亲　在千里之外
我们的骨肉　在水中
我们的鞋　埋在纤尘里
我们这一对双胞胎
不放纵　不拘束　甚少哭泣
头盔　还有异类目光
沉入水底　弟弟
我独爱千顷之野
如同心中旧识
水呀　淹过了膝盖

MY YOUNGER BROTHER IN THE WATER

Water   it's a room filled with waves
        it's a little bit sad
poured down from the sky into the perfume vial inside the body
I sniff the air
Catching a whiff of that chill
Seated here my beloved   Brother
To my right   a quick change of costume
O the water   has covered our toes

"I"   answer as if there were a small fruit in my mouth
Spat out it drives deep as a lance
Casting a glance   bright as a jewel
It's the trail
Brother   when the summer days press down   I want to
Draw a picture of myself with flowers in my hair
The spirit of my eyes   flows out the back of the paper
Shoots into the clouds   Could anyone be
More obsessively clean than that?
O the water   has covered our heels

Our parents   a thousand miles away
Our flesh and blood   in the water
Our shoes   deep in the dust of the road
We twins
Neither freed   nor bound   shedding few tears
Helmets   and inhuman eyes
Sink to the bottom of the water   Brother
I love only those wild acres
Like an old and intimate friend
O the water   is covering our knees

对畸形的事物嗜好
就像一个针眼　看不穿
又不知其深　弟弟
双眼和内心
都在贪馋地流泪
它们抖动泡沫　一匹一匹的
阳光布料　惊吓了
闷闷低飞的鸟
水呀　淹过了腰腹

弟弟　当冬日将至
刀刃已在闪光　冰霜的问候
躲在你的柔和嗓音里
"要"或者"不要"
伤了我　在这两叶

灰心的肺囊里　我呀
高举起熙熙攘攘的十根手指
不是投降　是向前
搅起一池哀嚎
水呀　淹过了胸腔

酽酒、修书、失睡
弟弟——不可测的度
驯服了前尘、后世和今生
他们洗一个澡　灭灯
然后相拥而眠　这一切
是自然的问题　弟弟
不是形而上的主题
也不仅仅是男女的问题
水呀　淹过了脖颈

A weakness for the grotesque
Like the eye of a needle   that you can't see through
And you can't know its depth   Brother
Your eyes and heart
Weeping with hunger
Tears that make the bubbles tremble   Bolt by bolt
Sunlight's fabric   startles
Listless birds flying low
O the water   has covered our waists

Brother   as winter approaches
The knife's blade is flashing   a frosty salutation
Lurking inside your gentle voice
"Will" or "Won't"
Have hurt me   In this pair of

Burnt-out lungs   O, I
Raise high my ten unruly fingers
It's not a surrender   but an advance
Stirring up a pool of lamentations
O the water   has covered our chests

Offering libations, compiling books, losing sleep
Brother — unfathomable depths
Have tamed the past, the future and this life
They bathe   quench the lamps
And fall asleep in each other's arms   All of this
Is a question of Nature   Brother
And not of metaphysics
Nor is it simply a problem between men and women
O the water   has risen to our necks

那深　是否触动了爱
那冷　帮助你
对天真　对热忱
不断研究　弟弟
我们的天性是遗传？
还是诗歌路过时
派生出的蜂蜜？
早晚饮一杯　对彼此有益
　　　　　黑暗中的鼻孔嗅到
那极端的甜……
水呀　淹过了头顶

That depth   does it move you to love
That cold   helps you
Ceaselessly probing   innocence
And zealotry   Brother
Is our nature something we inherit?
Or is it the honey that's distilled
When a poem passes by
Morning and evening we'll drink a cup   to our mutual health
       In the dark our nostrils flare and breathe in
The intense sweetness . . .
O the water   has covered our heads

吸管

每吸一下
我就颤抖一次
我的用力
吸干了你我之间的空气
吸管变得如此轻
它不该被如此挤压
它应该充满
蓝色的液体
假若我离我的力量远一点

STRAW

with every pull
I give a shudder
my effort
sucks the air between us dry
the straw becomes so light
too light to bear such pressure
it should be filled
with indigo liquid
if only I were farther from my own power

读报

每天晚上
　　他读到
　　　　一则凶杀新闻

　　（碎尸案　奶奶的自杀　毒血旺）
　　　　——此刻他睡意高涨
　　　　那些令人敬畏的消息
　　　　麻醉了他的每一寸肌肤

让我告诉你：
我的妻子是一个冒险家
她体内的万有引力
陡转直下

硫磺和砂金的热力
在我们头顶呼啸
子弹疯狂地夹紧　双臂的重量

　　　　　　　每个晚上　我们
在欢欣和恐惧中达至
极乐巅峰　"喂"的电话声
黄金和碎尸案会不会
一同爆炸？

READING THE NEWS

every night
      he comes across
            news of some awful murder

      (dismembered corpse   suicidal granny   poisoned hotpot)
            ——— just then he's flooded with the desire for sleep
            these horrifying stories
            have numbed every square inch of his skin

let me tell you:
my wife is a thrill-seeker
the universal gravitation of her body
plummeting suddenly

the heating power of sulphur and placer gold
scream from the crowns of our heads
bullets crazily pinching   the weight of our arms

      every evening   amidst this
terror and joy we reach
ecstatic peaks   the phone rings "hello"
will gold and the case of the dismembered corpse
explode in concert?

白日之眠

这是我们的白日之眠
　　　　他说，这时头朝上
　　　　脖子别无他用
　　　　除了亲吻　吮吸

镜子，梳子和赤裸的脚后跟
弯下了它们的尖状
　　　　全身的两半
　　　　一半写着：昼
　　　　一半写着：夜

（称呼你出自自然
　　呼你　助我直抵峰巅）

窗外
　　　　塔吊高高向我落下
　　　　辗转睡去　也无法闭上双眼

DAYLIGHT SLUMBERS

these are our daylight slumbers
        he says, right now we're looking up
        our necks have no other purpose
        besides kissing   sucking

the mirror, the comb and naked heels
hinge upon their points
        the two halves of a whole body
        one half inscribed: day
        the other: night

(calling you a child of nature
      calling you   to help me prop up this summit)

outside the window
        a tower crane falls towards me
        I toss and turn   but cannot shut my eyes in sleep

给吕德安

有人把信送到我的桌前
——正当纽约大雪时
我正在用一寸炭精条
挑出0.5寸的眉毛
以及0.3寸的美国式眼睛
（一般比中国人大）

至于我们的诗
却不像落满你全身的大片鹅毛
把我们变白　伪装成
各个市镇的美丽时光

在我的家乡（你的家乡也一样）
它们不常见　偶尔来临
因此要上报纸头条
它们细细飘零慢慢起飞
冬天那么多　它们却那么少
因此弥足珍贵　跟诗一样

FOR LÜ DE'AN

someone left a letter on my desktop
—— in the middle of a New York blizzard
just as I was using an inch of crayon
to pencil in half-inch wide eyebrows
and third-inch wide American-style eyes
(typically larger than Chinese eyes)

and as for our poems
they don't rain down and bury you like big puffs of goose down
turning us white   disguising us
as beautiful interludes in each small town

in my hometown (and in yours too)
they're seldom seen   when they do appear
they're front page news
so very fine, they swirl and drift, borne slowly aloft
so many winters   but they are still as rare
and precious   as poetry

催眠术

她告诉我　人的一生
都密封在
自己的睡眠里

她的手势　她的语气
还有全世界的一生
都提供给我
一分钟的深深倦意

她吐气如兰　向
大脑中的松果腺体
我昏昏欲睡时
看到了前世的蝴蝶

回去　回不去
我的前半辈子
在睡眠中厮杀　她发现
我的灵魂
服用了　世纪末的褪黑素

HYPNOSIS

she tells me   your entire life
is locked inside
your sleep

her gestures   her tone of voice
and the life of all the world
bestow on me
a moment of profound exhaustion

the sweetness of her breath   insinuates
itself into my pineal gland
as sleep overtakes me
I see a butterfly from a previous existence

going back   yet unable
the first half of my life
struggles desperately in my sleep   she discovers
my spirit
has dosed itself   with millenial melatonin

天敌

他，猛地，从空中
摔下自己

我抬了抬眼镜
看见，两条身影

她的，盔甲
一向是黑夜

他把她变成
僵硬的一条

因为
他们是天敌

我继续蜷缩在
纸上　那些字

渐渐变成猫与鼠的厮拼
现在　我比它们更小

不知道我的天敌
是否相信

NATURAL ENEMIES

violently, from the sky, he
hurls himself down

I adjust my glasses and look
up, a pair of silhouettes

hers, armored
as ever in night

he turns her
into something rigid

because
they are natural enemies

I persist in twisting
on paper   these words

it's evolving into a fatal game of cat and mouse
now   I'm even smaller than they are

and I wonder if my natural enemy
is not faith itself

我醉，你不喝

杯子如约而来时
你不醉　那谁肯
握住一个险恶的漩涡
还有它的必然？

我所看到的突然的微笑
那么小　那么聪明
是因为我埋在醉里

所有的酒精都怕我
因此夜晚　最值得
蹈入险境　去取走醉里的
化学反应　比熟悉我的
香水品牌　你还熟悉
我偷走的每一道目光

突然我慢慢变红
而你也变得更蓝
如果不是乙醇　那就得
是一个伤口
它们补充你被不醉
轻轻吸走的功力

爱如同酒
有人闻它　有人饮
它才存在　它才滴滴见血
才让人心痛　才会在醉里
相信某个人的怪念头

I'M DRUNK AND YOU'RE DRY

the glass arrives right on time
you're not drunk   but who'd want to
grasp so treacherous a vortex?
and what's the point, anyway?

the instant smiles I see
are so faint   so intelligent
because I'm awash in my own drunkenness

every kind of alcohol fears me
that's why nighttime   is best
for going out on a limb   for snatching from drunkenness
that chemical reaction   you know well
my perfume   and know even better
each and every glance I've stolen

suddenly I'm flushing red
but you get bluer all the time
if it isn't alcohol   it must be
a wound
shoring up the strength
your sobriety softly sucks away

love is like wine
some breathe its vapors   while others imbibe
and bring it into existence   and let it draw blood
and bring us pain   only intoxication
lets us place our faith in another's folly

现在我要它像个生命
而不只是生活的附件
我用什么来养它？
药物，食物，性物？

我不愿等待的后果
已开始鼓掌

终究要变成红人了
0.5寸高的酒要就见底了
你不喝，我醉得更快

right now I want it to be like life itself
and not just an accessory to living
but what can I nurture it with?
drugs, food, sex?

the effect I was impatient for
gives a round of applause

I'm turning into a lush
a half-inch of liquor away from the bottom of the glass
you're not drinking, and I get drunker all the time

烟花的寂寞

烟花与烟花女子
都有过狂欢起舞
最终，她们落入寂寞

道学家们不会同意：
她们在天上的爆破多么自然
我们随便看　随便想
就被照亮了　不曾经意的角落

假如我的意志也可以升空
我也想四分五裂
为了求爱　笔直起舞
每个人都会　对着月亮狂乱
月亮也酷爱自己的极乐

假如可能
它也会引爆自己
从每一个方向
洒出全身的花朵骨头

FIREWORKS AND WORKING GIRLS

Fireworks and working girls
They've danced with abandon
Descending into loneliness in the end

A moralist would not agree:
Their explosions in the heavens are natural
We watch as we please   reflect as we please
On newly illuminated   corners once overlooked

If my will could ascend to the sky
I'd want to go to pieces too
In the quest for love   I'd dance a proud dance
Anyone might   surrender to lust beneath the moon
Even the moon adores its own ecstasy

If it were able
It would light its own fuse
Every flowery bone of its body
Scattering to the winds

终于使我周转不灵

我的灵魂比我的舌头
跑得快　我的手
比我的心　敏感善变

就让我们来演奏
四重唱吧

又来了一个人校音

好端端的一整天
你谋杀了我的嗓子
从温柔的资讯　到沙哑的排练
你终于使我周转不灵

现在轮到我来演奏！
我和我心爱的旋律
滔滔不绝　我们要
拷贝一片黄金

我要修理我的灵魂
让它更骨感
我要抓住我的呼吸跑动
离开和回来
我要追赶你的吐字均匀
还要你相信我的发音
和　对恋人的第六感应

你终于使我周转不灵

IN THE END I COME UP SHORT

Compared to my tongue my spirit
Runs fast   my hands
Are flightier and more fretful   than my heart

So let's all get up and sing
A quartet

And here comes someone to keep us in tune

It was a perfectly fine day
And you came along and killed my voice
Taking it from a soft murmur   to a ragged drone
You've made me come up short

Now it's my turn to perform!
Me and my beloved melody
Pouring out   we will
Copy down a piece of gold

I want to reshape my soul
Into something bonier
I want to catch my rushing breath
As it comes and goes
I want to keep up with the even cadences of your words
Want you to believe in the sound of mine
And   in the sixth sense I have for my beloved

You've made me come up short in the end

它们总是如此

有些梦　不同于很美的梦
关于摩托车
加油站和蹂躏
类似我们看惯的暴力片

它们总是这样飞来飞去
它们这些暴力
它们总是又温柔又铺张
像一个美学

他们赤裸　他们兴奋
他们在白色床单下
狂野　或者温柔
都轻如鸿毛
他们发誓　他们言必称爱
他们在说服自己　还是对方？
这一夜产生了怀疑

它们总是这样
美与不美　它们总是这样
进入我们的大脑
它们总是这样站在一起
把我们毁掉

太阳不应该嫉妒
它之下的一切光芒
太阳不应该照亮
围绕美的全部事实

THINGS ARE ALWAYS LIKE THAT

Some dreams   unlike beautiful dreams
Are all about motorcycles
Gas stations and mayhem
Like the violent movies we're used to watching

They're always flying around
Their kind of violence
Is at once gentle and grandiose
Like an aesthetic

They're naked   they're excited
Beneath white sheets
Wild   or tender
Light as cranes' feathers
They make a pledge   whenever they talk they'll talk about love
Are they convincing themselves   or trying to convince each other
Tonight I've started to wonder

Things are always like that
Beautiful or not   they're always the same
Entering our brains
Always standing together in the same way
Dragging us down

The sun shouldn't be jealous
Of the rays of light beneath it
The sun shouldn't shine
On the realities that encircle beauty

有些梦　总是杀机毕现
盖过月黑的时候
总是成为经典
类似我们看惯的暴力片

它们总是这样
它们在黑夜里嘎嘎生长
它们代表我们身体的骨骼
要是欢爱如此巨大
它们就代表我们的怀疑

杀人时不会想到有瘾
就像下毒时不会想到死
爱人时也不会想到明年今天

Some dreams   always reveal their murderous intent
For in the dark of the moon
They'll always become classics
Like the violent movies we're used to watching

Things are always like that
They bump around in the dead of night
And speak for the bones in our bodies
If delight were as vast as that
They would speak for our doubts as well

You can kill without meaning to make it a habit
Swallow poison without thinking of death
Fall in love and never wonder what the year might bring

菊花灯笼漂过来

菊花一点点漂过来
在黑夜　在周围的静
在河岸沉沉的童声里
菊花淡　淡出鸟影

儿童提着灯笼漂过来
他们浅浅的合唱里
没有恐惧　没有嬉戏　没有悲苦
只有菊花灯笼　菊花的淡
灯笼的红

小姐也提着灯笼漂过来
小姐和她的仆从
她们都挽着松松的髻
她们的华服盛装　不过是
丝绸　飘带和扣子
不过是走动时窸窣乱响的
璎珞　耳环　钗凤

小姐和小姐的乳娘
她们都是过来人
她们都从容地寻找
在夜半时面对月亮
小姐温柔　灯笼也温柔
她们漂啊漂
她们把平凡的夜
变成非凡的梦游

每天晚上
菊花灯笼漂过来

CHRYSANTHEMUM LANTERNS GO FLOATING BY

Chrysanthemums go floating by, dot after dot
Through the darkness   through the enclosing silence
Past the muffled voices of children by the river
Pale chrysanthemums   paleness startling the shadows of birds

Children holding lanterns float slowly by
In their shallow singing
There is no fear   no play   no pain
Only chrysanthemum lanterns   the paleness of chrysanthemums
The crimson of lanterns

And young ladies holding lanterns float slowly by
Young ladies and their servants
Hair tied in loose knots
All of their finery   is nothing but
Satin   sashes and buttons
Nothing but jingling and jangling
Tassels   earrings   phoenix hairpins

The young ladies and their nursemaids
They're passers-by
They're seeking in their leisurely way
A midnight rendezvous with the moon
The girls are gentle   the lanterns gentle too
They float, o they float
They turn an ordinary night
Into an extraordinary walking dream

Every night
Chrysanthemum lanterns float slowly by

菊花灯笼的主人　浪迹天涯
他忽快忽慢的脚步
使人追不上
儿童们都跟着他成长

　　这就是沧海一灯笼的故事

　　如果我坐在地板上
　　我会害怕那一股力量
　　我会害怕那些菊影　光影　人影
　　我也会忽快忽慢
　　在房间里丁当作响

　　如果我坐在沙发或床头
　　我就会欣赏
　　我也会感到自己慢慢透明
　　慢慢变色
　　我也会终夜含烟　然后
　　离地而起

The master of lanterns   wanders far and wide
No one can keep up with
His uneven pace, now fast now slow
The children grow up in his footsteps

This is the tale of a lantern on the deep blue sea

If I were sitting on the floor
I would feel afraid of that breath of power
I would feel afraid of those blossom shadows   light shadows
                    human shadows
And I would give voice, now fast now slow
Ringing like a bell in the room

Sitting on the sofa or the bed
It would put me at ease
And I'd feel myself slowly turning translucent
Slowly changing color
Holding the smoke inside me all night   And then
I'd float up from the ground

重阳登高

——遍插茱萸少一人

思亲问题　友爱问题
一切问题中最动人的
全都是登高的问题
都是会当凌绝顶时
把盏的问题

今朝一人　我与谁长谈？
遥望远处　据称是江北
白练入川是一条，还是两条？
汇向何处　都让我喜欢

在江北以远　是无数美人
男人们登高　都想得到她们
尽管千年之内　哺乳动物
和人类　倒一直
保持着生态平衡

今朝我一人把盏　江山变色
青色三春消耗了我
九九这个数字　如今又要
轮回我的血脉
远处一俯一仰的山峰
赤裸着跳入我怀中
我将只有毫无用处地
享受艳阳

CLIMBING THE HEIGHTS ON THE DOUBLE NINTH

— People all around adorned
with flowers, but someone is missing

The problem of longing for family   the problem of brotherly love
The most touching problem of all is
Climbing the heights
When you've reached a pinnacle
And raise a cup

Today I am alone   who is there to talk to?
Taking in a distant view   what people call the North Bank
Is that a single white ribbon joining the River, or are there two?
Wherever those twined currents go   I'll be content

Beyond the North Bank   are beautiful women without number
Every man who climbs these heights   will think of them
Even if in the next thousand years   mammals
And humans   merge into one
Maintaining the balance of Nature

Today I raise a cup alone   while River and mountains change color
The green months of spring depleted me
This figure, "Nine Nine"   is once again
Reborn in my veins
Faraway peaks above and below
Plunge naked into my heart
It's useless but all I can do is
Enjoy the glorious sunshine

思伤脾　醉也伤脾
飒飒风声几万？呼应谁来临？
饮酒入喉　它落到身体最深处
情欲和生死问题
离别和健康问题
也入喉即化　也落到最深处
它们变得敏捷　又绵密
它们醉了　也无处不在

Longing is miserable   Being drunk is miserable too
How many sighs in the soughing of the wind?   Who will answer
                                                                                my echo?
Wine poured down the throat   flows into the body's deepest reaches
Problems of desire and mortality
Problems of separation and health
Also change inside the throat   and flow into the body's deepest reaches
They become nimble   yet meticulous
They're drunk   and they're everywhere

Zhai Yongming notes that she wrote this poem after climbing Xisha Mountain in Nanjing on the Double Ninth. The Double Ninth is a festival that takes place every autumn, on the ninth day of the ninth lunar month. The original meaning of the festival may have been related to driving away bad luck, but it has long been an occasion for outings, especially hikes in the hills to some viewpoint, for chrysanthemum viewing, and for drinking chrysanthemum wine. Traditionally, people also wore zhuyu flowers on this day, for good luck. The epigram is taken from a poem by the Tang dynasty poet, Wang Wei (699–759 CE), "Missing My Shandong Brothers on the Ninth Day of the Ninth Month" (九月九日忆山东兄弟).

潜水艇的悲哀

9点上班时
我准备好咖啡和笔墨
再探头看看远处打来
第几个风球
有用或无用时
我的潜水艇都在值班
铅灰的身体
躲在风平的浅水塘

开头我想这样写：
如今战争已不太来到
如今诅咒　也换了方式
当我监听　能听见
碎银子哗哗流动的声音

鲜红的海鲜　仍使我倾心
艰难世事中　它愈发通红
我们吃它　掌握信息的手在穿梭
当我开始写　我看见
可爱的鱼　包围了造船厂

国有企业的烂账　以及
邻国经济的萧瑟　还有
小姐趋时的妆容
这些不稳定的收据　包围了
我的浅水塘

于是我这样写道：
还是看看
我的潜水艇　最新在何处下水

THE SUBMARINE'S LAMENT

starting work at 9 am
I ready my coffee my pen
poking my head outside to check on the latest
typhoon warning
whether I need it or not
my submarine is always ready
its lead gray body
hiding beneath the windless surface of a shallow pool

at first I wanted to write this:
currently the war hasn't touched us
currently curses   are taking a different tack
from my listening post   I hear
the gentle rush of silvery fragments

crimson shellfish   still catch my fancy
in the tumult of world events   it flushes a deeper red
and we eat it   the hand grasping the data shuttles back and forth
when I start writing   I see
cute little fish   encircling the shipyard

state enterprises are going under   what's more
there's economic panic next door   and those
girls with stylish painted faces
these volatile receipts   encircle
our shallow pool

so this is what I write:
let me see
where should I launch   my submarine this time

在谁的血管里泊靠
追星族，酷族，迪厅的重金属
分析了写作的潜望镜

酒精，营养，高热量
好像介词，代词，感叹词
锁住我的皮肤成分
潜水艇　它要一直潜到海底
紧急　但又无用地下潜
再没有一个口令可以支使它

从前我写过　现在还这样写：
都如此不适宜了
你还在造你的潜水艇
它是战争的纪念碑
它是战争的坟墓　它将长眠海底
但它又是离我们越来越远的
适宜幽闭的心境

正如你所看到的：
现在　我已造好潜水艇
可是　水在哪儿
水在世界上拍打
现在　我必须造水
为每件事物的悲伤
制造它不可多得的完美

in whose veins will it weigh anchor
the starstruck, the hipsters, heavy metal in discos
analyzing the periscope of writing

alcohol, nourishment, high in calories
as if prepositions, pronouns, exclamations
were sealing up portions of my skin
submarine   it will plunge to the bottom of the sea
urgently   but it's diving for nothing
no longer subject to orders

I've written this before, and I'll write it again:
it doesn't add up
you're still building your submarine
that memorial to war
that tomb of the war dead   lying dormant at the bottom of the sea
but it grows ever more distant over time
in its self-imposed isolation

you can see for yourself:
that now   I've built my submarine
and yet   where is the water
it's lapping over the world
and now   I must create water
and fashion an elusive wholeness
for the lament that lies in everything

轻伤的人，重伤的城市

轻伤的人过来了
他们的白色纱布像他们的脸
他们的伤痕比战争缝合得好
轻伤的人过来了
担着心爱的东西
没有断气的部分
脱掉军服　洗净全身
使用支票和信用卡

一个重伤的城市血气翻涌
脉搏和体温在起落
比战争快
比恐惧慢
重伤的城市
扔掉了假腿和绷带
现在它已流出绿色分泌物
它已提供石材的万能之能
一个轻伤的人　仰头
看那些美学上的建筑

六千颗炸弹砸下来
留下一个燃烧的军械所
六千颗弹着点
像六千只重伤之眼
匆忙地映照出
那几千个有夫之妇
有妇之夫　和未婚男女的脸庞
他们的身上全是硫磺，或者沥青
他们的脚下是拆掉的钢架

LIGHTLY INJURED PEOPLE,
GRAVELY WOUNDED CITY

Here they come, the lightly injured
Their gauze as white as their faces
Wounds sewn up better than the war's
Here they come, the lightly injured
Carrying their prized possessions
The parts that have not died
They strip off their uniforms   they wash themselves clean
Paying by check and credit card

The gravely wounded city seethes with energy
Its pulse and temperature rise and fall
Faster than war
Slower than fear
Casting off its bandages and artificial legs
It has bled green fluid
And offered the unyielding power of stone
One of the lightly injured   looks up
At those monuments to aesthetics

Six thousand bombs come pounding down
Leaving an arms depot in flames
Six thousand bomb craters
Like six thousand gravely wounded eyes
In a rush they illuminate the faces of
Thousands of married women
Married men   unmarried men and women
Bodies covered in sulphur   or asphalt
And at their feet, twisted metal

轻伤的人　从此
拿着一本重伤的地图
他们分头去寻找那些
新的器皿大楼
薄形，轻形和尖形
这个城市的脑袋
如今尖锐锋利地伸出去
既容易被砍掉
也吓退了好些伤口

The lightly injured   now set out
Heavily wounded maps in hand
They split up to search
For the new vessels of tall buildings
Forms thin and light and pointed
The brain of this city
Extends its spikes
So easily hacked off
But they've frightened away many wounds

她的视点

她的视点从床的一端
射向另一端　看着你的身体
从一大堆衣服　手机　鞋
和钥匙中钻出来

还有你的指头
它们修长　刚直
似乎能再次听见
骨盆和白昼的碰撞声

每个人都被阉割了
每个人的健康都遗失了
每个人都暴露在他的肉体之外

要去的地方是个苦难窝
即使穿上盔甲　此时也不能
把你的穴道包裹起来
你的每一寸肌肤终究会
慵懒起来　可供抚摸
她也会为此快活一番

关灯吧　进化论的高潮一再说:
你今晚准备献出来的
不是那么重要　对她而言

(他们的孩子会看见
生育的全过程
羊水　血　婴儿
唏里哗啦地冲出来
没留下一滴精子可供选择
没留下一寸空间可供栖息)

HER POINT OF VIEW

From one side of the bed, her point of view
Looking through the opposite side   watching your body
Emerging from a heap of clothing   cell phone   shoes
And keys

And let's not forget your fingers
They're long, slender   and straight
It's as if we could hear once again
The collision of hipbones and daylight

Everyone's been desexed
Everyone's unhealthy
Everyone's exposed outside their flesh

The place you're headed is a slough of despond
Even your suit of armor   cannot
Protect your pressure points this time
Every square inch of your skin
Will grow slack in the end   Perhaps a little stroking
Might give her some pleasure as well

Turn out the lights   The climax of evolutionary theory repeats ad nauseam:
What you're about to offer up tonight
Isn't that important   as far as she's concerned

(Their child could witness
The entire process of procreation
Amniotic fluid   blood   baby
As it all comes splashing out there's
Nothing left behind, not one drop of semen
Nothing left behind, no space to call a haven)

时间美人之歌

某天与朋友偶坐茶园
谈及，开元、天宝
那些盛世年间
以及纷乱的兵荒年代

当我年轻的时候
我四处寻找作诗的题材
我写过战争、又写过女人的孤单
还有那些磨难，加起来像椎子
把我的回忆刺穿
我写呀写，一直写到中年

我看见了一切
在那个十五之夜：
一个在盘子上起舞的女孩
两个临风摆动的影子
四周爱美的事物——
向她倾斜的屋檐
对她呼出万物之气的黄花
鼓起她裙裾的西风　然后才是

　　　那注视她舞蹈之腿的
　　　几乎隐蔽着的人

　　　月圆时，我窥见这一切
　　　真实而又确然
　　　一个簪花而舞的女孩
　　　她舞，那月光似乎把她穿透
　　　她舞，从脚底那根骨头往上
　　　她舞，将一地落叶拂尽

THE SONG OF HISTORICAL BEAUTIES

Sitting in a tea garden with a friend one day
Our talk turned to Kaiyuan and Tianbao
That gilded age
Those days of chaos and strife

When I was young
I searched high and low for things to write about
I wrote of war, of women's loneliness
And about hardships that came together like an awl
Piercing my memory
And I write and write, writing myself into middle age

I saw the entire thing
That night, the 15th of the lunar month:
A girl dancing on a platter
A pair of shadows swaying in the breeze
Surrounded by admirers —
The eaves inclining towards her
Golden chrysanthemums wafting the scent of all creation towards her
The West wind lifting her skirt and sash   and then

    Someone nearly hidden
    Transfixed by her dancing legs

    Under a full moon, I watch it all
    Unquestionably real
    A dancing girl with flowers in her hair
    She dances, the moonlight seeming to pass right through her
    She dances, movement flowing up from the bones in the soles of her feet
    She dances, sweeping away the fallen leaves

(她不关心宫廷的争斗)
她只欲随风起舞、随风舞)

四周贪婪的眼光以及
爱美的万物
就这样看着她那肉体的全部显露

当我年轻的时候
少数几个人还记得
我那些诗的题材
我写过疾病、童年和
黑暗中的所有烦恼
我的忧伤蔑视尘世间的一切
我写呀写，一直写到中年

我的确看到过一些战争场面：
狼烟蔽日，剑气冲天
帅字旗半卷着四面悲歌
为何那帐篷里传出凄凉的歌咏？

一杯酒倒进了流光的琥珀酒盏
一个女人披上了她的波斯软甲
是什么使得将军眼含泪花？
是什么使得绝代美女惊恐万状？

(她不关心乌骓马嘶鸣的意义
她只愿跟随着它，跟随他)

除了今夜古老的月亮以及
使我毛发直竖的寒风
还有谁？注视着这一堆
淤血和尸骨混合的影象

(She gives no thought to palace intrigues
Desiring only to dance with the wind, to dance with the wind)

Surrounded by hungry eyes and
The admiration of all creation
Watching as her flesh is laid bare

Very few people remember
What I wrote about
When I was young
I wrote of illness, of childhood
My darkest days and all their troubles
In my misery, I looked down on this mundane world
And I wrote and wrote, writing myself into middle age

I can say I've witnessed scenes of warfare:
Smoke swallowing the sun, blades piercing the sky
The generals' standards half furled, dirges filling the air
Why do we hear such mournful songs outside the tent?

A glass of wine is poured into a shining amber cup
A woman dons her soft Persian armor
What makes the general's eyes fill with tears?
What makes that peerless beauty quake in fear?

(She gives no thought to the neighing of the emperor's horses,
Wanting only to be with him, to be with him)

Tonight, apart from the ancient moon
And a chill wind that raises the hairs on the back of my neck,
Who else is there? Eyes fixed on this mound
Of images of spilled blood and broken bones

当我年轻的时候
我丢下过多少待写的题材
我写过爱情、相思和
一个男人凝视的目光　唯独没有写过衰老
我写呀写，一直写到中年

　　西去数里，温泉山中
　　浮动着暗香的热汤
　　一件丝绸袍子叠放在地上

　　西去数里，勒马停缰
　　厌战的将士一声呐喊
　　黑暗中总有人宣读她们的罪状

　　西去数里，逃亡途中
　　和泪的月光
　　一根玉钗跌落在地上

　　(她听不见动地的鼙鼓声
　　她听见绵绵私语，绵绵誓)

　　千军万马曾踏过这个温泉
　　那水依然烫，依然香
　　后世的爱情，刚出世的爱情
　　依然不停地涌出，出自那个泉眼

　　某天与朋友偶坐茶园
谈及纷纷来去的盛世年间
我已不再年轻，也不再固执
将事物的一半与另一半对立
我睁眼看着来去纷纷的人和事

When I was young
I had so many ideas that never saw the light of day
I've written of love, of longing and
The steady gaze of a man   The only thing I haven't written
                about is growing old
Writing and writing, writing myself into middle age

    Some miles westward they ride, to hot springs in the hills
    To soak in that faintly fragrant water
    A silk gown folded on the ground

    Some miles westward they ride, reining in their mounts to a halt
    War-weary officers and men call out for blood
    There's always someone in the shadows, denouncing women for
      their crimes

    Some miles westward they ride, and as they flee
    The moon weeps with them
    A jade hairpin tumbles to the ground

    (She doesn't hear the rumble of war drums shaking the earth
    She hears the unbroken flow of whispers, unbroken strings of oaths)

    Legions of soldiers and thousands of horses have trod past these springs
    Their waters are as warm as ever, and just as sweet
    Love after death, and love newly born
    Well up from that source, as they always have

    I was sitting with a friend in a tea garden one day
And our talk turned to how swiftly golden ages come and go
I'll never be young again, never again be so willful
As to pit one half of creation against the other
I watch with wonder the flurry of people and things as they come and go

时光从未因他们，而迟疑或停留
我一如既往地写呀写
我写下了这样的诗行：

"当月圆之夜
由于恣情的床笫之欢
他们的骨头从内到外地发酥
男人呵男人
开始把女人叫作尤物
而在另外的时候
当大祸临头
当城市开始燃烧
男人呵男人
乐于宣告她们的罪状"

Time has neither paused nor stopped, not for any of them
I keep on writing, just as I always have
And these are the lines I wrote:

> **"One night, under a full moon**
> **They abandoned themselves to passion**
> **Leaving their bodies limp to the core**
> **Men, oh men**
> **At first they praise a woman for her beauty**
> **But at other times**
> **When catastrophe looms**
> **When cities erupt in flames**
> **Men, oh men**
> **Delight in denouncing women for their crimes"**

Tang Xuanzong (685–762) reigned from 712 to 756. The Kaiyuan period of his reign spanned the years 713–741, and the Tianbao period spanned the years 742–756.

This poem alludes to three legendary and historic beauties: Zhao Feiyan (c. 32 BCE–1 BCE), an empress of the Western Han; Yu Ji (died 202 BCE), consort of Xiang Yu of Chu; and Yang Guifei (719–756), consort of the Tang Emperor Xuanzong. All three women were vilified by traditional historians.

关于雏妓的一次报道

雏妓又被称作漂亮宝贝
她穿着花边蕾丝小衣
大腿已是撩人
她的妈妈比她更美丽
她们像姐妹　"其中一个像羚羊"……

男人都喜欢这样的宝贝
宝贝也喜欢对着镜头的感觉

我看见的雏妓却不是这样
她12岁　瘦小而且穿着肮脏
眼睛能装下一个世界
或者　根本已装不下哪怕一滴眼泪

她的爸爸是农民　年轻
但头发已花白
她的爸爸花了三个月
一步一步地去寻找他
失踪了的宝贝

雏妓的三个月
算起来快100多天
300多个男人
这可不是简单数
她一直不明白为什么
那么多老的，丑的，脏的男人
要趴在她的肚子上
她也不明白这类事情本来的模样
只知道她的身体

148

REPORT ON A CHILD PROSTITUTE

Some people call a child prostitute pretty baby
She wears lacy embroidered lingerie
Her thighs already inviting
Her mother is even prettier
They look like sisters   "But she is the gazelle . . ."

Men love a pretty baby
And she loves gazing at herself in the mirror

But the child I saw wasn't like that
She's twelve years old   thin and dressed in rags
Her eyes take in the entire world
And perhaps   there's not room for even a single tear

Her father is a peasant   he's young
But his hair is already gray
He's spent three months already
Searching everywhere for his
Lost baby

Three months for a child prostitute
That's nearly 100 days
Over 300 men
Not an easy number for a child
She's never understood why
So many old, ugly, filthy men
Want to press themselves to her belly
She doesn't understand what it's all about
She only knows her body

变轻变空　被取走某些东西
雏妓又被认为美丽无脑
关于这些她一概不知
她只在夜里计算
她的算术本上有 300多个
无名无姓　　无地无址的形体
他们合起来称作消费者
那些数字像墓地里的古老符号
太阳出来以前　　消失了

看报纸时我一直在想：
不能为这个写诗
不能把诗变成这样
不能把诗嚼得嘎蹦直响
不能把词敲成牙齿　去反复啃咬
那些病　那些手术
那些与12岁加在一起的统计数字

诗、绷带、照片、回忆
刮伤我的眼球
(这是视网膜的明暗交接地带)
一切全表明:都是无用的
都是无人关心的伤害
都是每一天的数据　它们
正在创造出某些人一生的悲哀

部分地她只是一张新闻照片
12岁　　与别的女孩站在一起
你看不出　她少一个卵巢
一般来说　那只是报道
每天　我们的眼睛收集成千上万的资讯
它们控制着消费者的欢愉
它们一掠而过　"它"也如此

Is becoming light and empty   that something's been taken from it
Some people think child prostitutes are pretty but dumb
But she wouldn't know about that
She spends her nights counting
She counts over 300
Nameless figures   residence unknown
Collectively they're consumers
Their numbers like ancient symbols in a graveyard
Vanishing   before dawn

Reading the paper I keep thinking:
You can't write a poem about this
You can't turn poetry into something like this
You can't chew up a poem
Or hammer words into teeth   to eat away
These diseases   these incisions
These large sums added to her twelve years

Poem, bandage, photo, memory
They scratch at my eyes
(Here in the retinal zone where dark and light meet)
Everything becomes clear: it's useless
No one cares about this damage
It's just a daily quotient   of data
Creating a life of misery for someone else

In part she's just a picture in the paper
12 years old   standing in a group of girls
You can't see   she's missing an ovary
You could say   it's just a story in the news
Every day   our eyes take in thousands of pieces of information
That control our pleasure as consumers
That stream past us   just like this item

信息量　热线　和国际视点
像巨大的麻布　抹去了一个人卑微的伤痛

我们这些人　　看了也就看了
它被揉皱　　塞进黑铁桶里

Masses of information   hotlines   global perspectives
Like a huge rough rag   wiping away one person's feeble suffering

People like us   take a glance and that's all
Crumple up the paper   stuff it in a metal bin

五十年代的语言

生于五十年代　我们说的
就是这种语言
如今　它们变成段子
在晚宴上　被一道一道地
端了上来

那些红旗、传单
暴戾的形象　那些
双手紧扣的皮带
和嗜血的口号　已僵硬倒下
那些施虐受虐的对象
他们不再回来
而整整一代的爱情　已被阉割
也不再回来

生于五十年代　　但
我们已不再说那些语言
正如我们也不再说"爱"
所有的发声、词组和语气
都在席间跳跃着发黄

他们都不懂　他们年轻的发丝
在阳光下斑斓　象香皂泡
漂浮在我的身边
他们的脑袋一律低垂着
他们的姆指比其它手指繁忙
短信息　QQ　还有一种象形字母:
生于五十年代
我们也必须学会　在天上飞奔的语言

THE LANGUAGE OF THE '50S

Born in the '50s   that's the language
We speak
These days   it's the stuff of stand-up
At dinner parties   where it's served
Line by line

Those red flags, leaflets
Violent images   those
Belts pulled taught by stalwart thumbs
And those bloodthirsty slogans   have been brought down hard
The victimizers and victims
Are gone for good
The love of an entire generation   has been castrated
Gone for good

Born in the '50s   but
We'll never use that language again
Just as we'll never say "love" again
Every act of speech, each phrase and tone
Capers about yellowed with age at dinner parties

None of them understands   their youthful hair
Shines multicolored in the sun   like soap bubbles
Floating beside us
They bow their heads in unison
Their thumbs busier than their other digits
Texting on   QQ   and there's a symbolic typography too:
Born in the '50s
We too need to learn   that language flying around the ether

所有那些失落的字词
只在个别时候活过来
它们象撒帐时落下的葡萄、枸杞和大枣
落在了我们的床第之间
当我喃喃自语　一字一字地说出
我的男友听懂了　它们
因此变得猩红如血

All of those vanished words
Lived at a particular time
Like the grapes, wolfberries and dates scattered on our marriage bed
They fall between the sheets
And when I murmur   speaking each word one by one
My boyfriend understands   and they
Turn the vivid red of blood

胡惠姗自述

——感谢刘家琨叔叔
修建了胡惠姗纪念馆
我的同学谁来纪念？

他们躺在何处　我找不着
他们的名字再也无人知道
他们也有父母　父母也像火焰般燃烧
他们也有脐带　脐带把父母的命
往地下缠绕
他们一样也有乳牙　再也无人收藏

再也没有第二所学校　能让我们入读
再也没有　天堂里也没有
再也没有人间父母为我流泪
再也没有　天堂里也没有

这是世界上最长的裂缝
把我们一併吞下　剩下的
只有数字庞大　大到让更大数目的人流泪

当纪念我的水泥标号
超过学校　我瘦小的身体
能否把强壮的大地抬起
我能否翻个身　把地底的能量送出去
让上面的人看到

THE TESTAMENT OF HU HUISHAN

— with gratitude to Uncle Liu Jiakun
who built a memorial to Hu Huishan;
but who will make memorials
for all my classmates?

Where do they lie   I cannot find them
No one remains who knows their names
They too had mothers and fathers   mothers and fathers who also
                                        burned like flames
They too had umbilical cords   umbilical cords that took their
                                       parents' lives
Winding towards the ground
They too had milk teeth   but no one remains to save them

There won't be another school   where we might study
It's gone forever   and it's not in Heaven
Nor is there a mother or father to weep for me
They're gone forever   and they're not in Heaven

This is the longest fissure on the face of the earth
It swallowed us all   and all that remains
Are huge numbers   numbers large enough to make an even greater
                                        number of people weep

When the grade of concrete used for my memorial
Is better than that of my school could my frail body
Lift up the mighty earth
Could I turn my body   and release energy from underground
So people on the surface would see

整个班级的身体都压在这里
男女同学的躯体冒出
象石缝里的鲜花 冒出最后的鲜美
一声不响的我们
已不能让某些人看见
曾经是怎样的能量 把学校变成废墟

我能感觉到：在我头上
人们已不再疼痛 除了我父母
大地已不再震颤 除了偶尔的闪电
花重开 清风重来 歌又唱
再也没有了为时两月的愤怒

我叫胡惠姗
生于92年10月11日
没于2008年5月12日下午2:28分
享年15岁零6个月23天，
火化时间2008年5月15日

我叫胡惠姗
生前喜欢文学，梦想成为作家
对父母而言 我留下的不多：
照片，书包，笔记本，乳牙，脐带……
对旁人而言，我什么也没留下

我叫胡惠姗
但愿我从未出生 从未被纪念
从未被父母抱在怀里
从未让他们如此悲痛
但愿依然美丽的 是15岁的笑脸
而不只是一个城市的名字

The bodies of my entire class lie crushed
The corpses of those boys and girls sticking out
Flowers in the crevices between stones   thrusting out their
                                        final bright beauty

We who are now silent
Can no longer show others
The sort of force   that turned our school to rubble

This I can feel: above my head
People are no longer suffering   except for my parents
The earth no longer quakes   except for chance flashes of lightning
Flowers will bloom again   cool breezes will blow again   songs will be sung
Those two months of anger are past

My name is Hu Huishan
Born October 11th, 1992
Died May 12th, 2008 at 2:28 in the afternoon
I lived for 15 years, 6 months and 23 days,
And was cremated on May 15th, 2008

My name is Hu Huishan
When I was alive I liked literature, and dreamed of becoming a writer
I haven't left much behind   for my mother and father:
Photographs, book bag, notebook, milk teeth, umbilicus . . .
I've left nothing for anyone else

My name is Hu Huishan
If only I'd never been born   never been mourned
Had never been held in my parents' arms
Had never caused them all this pain
If only the beauty that remained   was a 15-year-old's smiling face
Instead of just the name of a town

毕利烟

西川递给我一支毕利烟
十年前他抽过的毕利烟

毕利烟不是莫合烟
但如同莫合烟的味道一样
充满低层人民的性感

诗人们抽着毕利烟
想像这是贫民窟的味道
实际上　　我们住在使馆区
窗外绿茵如织　　绿孔雀踱步
乌鸦大而黑
扑向讨论圆桌上的　　"乌鸦嘴"

我们感到羞愧　　不只是写作苍白
不只是用印度语　泰语
中国语或孟加拉语
不只是讨论宗教问题　民族国家问题

如此多的问题不断被翻译
就像毕利烟不断被不同阶层的人
叼起、抽着、吸进
最后吐出来
一圈一圈去政治化的本土味道

BIDIS

Xi Chuan hands me a bidi
the same kind of cigarette he smoked ten years ago

Bidis aren't Xinjiang tobacco
but they taste just like it
recalling a low-class sexiness

The poets smoke bidis
imagining this is the smell of poor people's shacks
In fact   we're staying in the diplomatic quarter
with views of lush, verdant grounds   green peacocks pacing
huge, black crows
flapping towards the round conference table and   our magpie-like chattering

We're ashamed   not only because our writing is pallid
not only because everyone is speaking Hindi   Thai
Chinese or Bengali
not only because we're discussing religion   & nationalism

So many questions, all constantly being translated
while people from all walks of life are picking up bidis
taking a drag, inhaling
finally exhaling
ring by ring, driving away the smell of a politicized soil

Xi Chuan (b. 1963) is a leading contemporary poet in China. He was a member of the delegation that Zhai traveled with to India.

Bidis are a kind of cheap cigarette popular among India's poor. They are made of N. rustica rather than the less potent N. tabacum, which is most commonly used in cigarettes.

Thank you to the editors who published earlier versions of these poems in the following journals and anthologies:

"Desire": *Chicago Review*, Vol. 39, Nos. 3 & 4

"The Black Room": *The Temple* (1999), Vol. 3, No. 2

"Premonition" and "Revolving": *The Temple* (1999), Vol. 3, No. 4

"Daylight Slumbers" and "The Green Room": *Hayden's Ferry Review*, No. 41

"For Women Poets" and "Natural Enemies": *Twentieth-Century Chinese Women's Poetry: An Anthology,* Julia Lin, ed. (M.E. Sharpe, 2009)

"The Black Room" (revised version): *Language for a New Century: Contemporary Poetry from the Middle East, Asia, and Beyond*, Tina Chang, Natalie Handal, Ravi Shankar, eds. (Norton, 2008)

"For Women Poets", "Hypnosis", "Natural Enemies", "The Submarine's Lament", and "The Song of Lady Time" ("The Song of Historical Beauties"): *Full Tilt*, No. 3

"Fireworks and Working Girls", "Straw", "Hypnosis", "My Younger Brother in the Water", "My Bat", "In the End I Come Up Short", and "Eros": *Zoland Poetry*, No. 3

"Desire" and "Monologue": *The Frontier Tide* (Point Editions, 2009)

"Mother" and "Lightly Wounded People, Gravely Wounded City": *The Other Voice: International Poetry Nights in Hong Kong*, Gilbert C.F. Fong, Bei Dao, Shelby K.Y. Chan, eds. (The Chinese University Press, 2009)

"Mother" and "Lightly Injured People, Gravely Wounded City": *NEA/Copper Canyon* (2011)

"The Changing Room", "Reading the News", "Chrysanthemum Lanterns Go Floating By", and "The Language of the Fifties": *Mantis*, Josh Edwards, ed. (2011)

"Abandoned House", "Climbing the Heights on the Double Ninth", "I'm Drunk and You're Dry", "The Fifth Month" and "The Testament of Hu Huishan": *Cha: An Asian Literary Journal* (July 2011)

Jintian Series of Contemporary Literature

<u>Published Titles</u>
Flash Cards
Edited and Translated by Yu Jian, Wang Ping & Ron Padgett

<u>Upcoming Titles</u>
A Phone Call from Dalian
By Han Dong
Edited and Translated from Chinese by Nicky Harman, with Contributions from Maghiel
van Crevel, Michael Day, Tao Naikan, Tony Prince, and Yu Yan Chen
Introduction by Maghiel van Crevel

Doubled Shadows
By Ouyang Jianghe
Translated from Chinese by Austin Woerner